MEET JESUS IN THE SUNDAY GOSPELS

VOL. I

by

Anthony M. Coniaris

Meditations on the words of Jesus in the Sunday Gospel lessons of the Orthodox Church from February through July.

"In Him was life and the life was the light of men" (John 1:4).

Light and Life Publishing Company

Minneapolis, Minnesota

1986

Light and Life Publishing Company
P.O. Box 26421
Minneapolis, Minnesota 55426-0421

ISBN 0-937032-41-7

TABLE OF CONTENTS

Page

WE ARE
ACCOUNTABLE
The Second Coming of Jesus.
Matthew 25:31 - 46.

There is a great difference between our Seminary in Brookline (at least as I knew it) and an English University. At our Seminary students had to live by strict discipline. We could never skip class. We were obligated to spend a specified number of hours each day in study. We were required to attend chapel twice daily. We were not allowed to leave the grounds except at appointed times and by permission. Life at an English University, on the other hand, is the exact opposite. No one ever checks to see if the student is in class or not. There are no specified hours for study. Students come and go as they will. There are no requirements as to how late they can stay out, etc. Of course, there comes the time when the examination will reveal how each student has been putting in his time, but meanwhile they are free to do pretty much as they please.

When God created us with the power of free choice, He ordained that life should be more like that at an English university than at a seminary. God has given us a great amount of freedom. We can postpone or even refuse to perform our duty in life; we can choose to live by instinct or impulse. But God has ordained a time of examination, a time of judgment. One of the purposes of judgment will be to show how we have used the freedom, the time, the talents, the other blessings which God has lavished upon us. And on the results of that examination shall depend our eternal destiny.

As the "Titanic" was sinking, a woman sobbed in anguish as she climbed into a lifeboat, "If I had known this was going to happen, I'd have had the chocolate mousse for dessert!"

She was going to face her Maker in a few minutes and what she missed most was not having a chocolate mousse for dessert. Today we're going to talk about facing our Maker at the

Second Coming of Jesus not from the point of view of chocolate mousse but from the point of view of accountability.

One of the main lessons of the Gospel lesson today is that we are accountable in life for all that we say and do. And no one will ever be able to escape that accountability.

We heard Jesus say:

"When the Son of man comes in His glory, and all the angels with Him, then He will sit on His glorious throne. Before Him will be gathered all the nations, and He will separate them one from another as a shepherd separates the sheep from the goats . . ." (Matthew 25:31-32).

A Banquet of Consequences

Accountability is the name of the game for the Christian. No matter how hard we try, we cannot wash out on that one. It is there, whether we like it or not. St. Paul put it all into a few words which can be readily understood. "All of us must appear before Christ," he said, "to be judged by Him. Each one will receive what he deserves, according to everything he has done, good or bad, in his bodily life" (2 Cor. 5:10).

St. Paul felt strongly his own personal accountability to God. That is why he wrote to the Corinthians, "But with me it is a very small thing that I should be judged by you or by any human court. I do not even judge myself . . . it is the Lord Who judges me" (I Cor. 4:24).

Sooner or later everyone sits down to a banquet of consequences," wrote R. L. Stevenson. The One Who presides over and arranges this "banquet of consequences" is none other than the Lord of the Universe.

We reap precisely what we sow. As St. Paul writes,

"Do not be deceived. God is not mocked: for whatever a man sows, this he will also reap. For the one who sows to his own flesh will from the flesh reap corruption; but he who sows to the Spirit will from the Spirit reap eternal life" (Gal. 6:7-8).

It may not come soon . . . but it will come. When the bills come due, the wages of wilful sin are paid in full as are the

8

wages of the faithful. God may seem slow, but He doesn't compromise with consequences.

Records! Records!

Many records are kept for us in life: school records, military records, employment records, police records, credit records. And there is that record of our lives kept within our minds which never forget anything; everything is stored and filed in the unconscious. Jesus tells us that God also keeps records. One day these records will be opened. When they are, not one cup of cold water given in His name will be forgotten. Why does God keep records? Is it because He is sadistic and delights in meting out punishment? Of course not. It is because He cares about what we do. We matter to Him. If He did not love, He would not judge. Accountability is not based on God's punitive justice but on His love.

The Unpopular God

Of course, it is not too popular today to talk about God as Judge. The fashionable God today is all love and no judgment. Judgment is old-fashioned. People today want a God Who not only loves unconditionally, but also approves of us unconditionally. But being a loving God does not blind God to what is going on, nor does it make Him less honest in calling things as He sees them. The God Who created us; the God Who gave us all we have; the God Who sent His Son to the cross for our salvation, has expectations of us by which He measures our performance. We are accountable.

Should Anything Else Matter?

Each and every one of us will stand before God one day to be judged. Should anything else matter to us in life more than this? Should not every decision we make, every thought we think, every word we say, every deed we do be weighed in the light of this judgment?

Daniel Webster said once, ''The most important thought that ever occupied my mind was that of my individual responsibility to God.''

9

Let us look at accountability for a moment as it is practiced on the football field. A football team has eleven players. Each has his specific position on the team. As long as he is in the game, each player is bound to play his position to the very best of his ability. He is accountable for every movement he makes, and the success of the team depends on him. In much the same way we are accountable to God. He has given us our position in life. Ultimately we shall have to answer to Him for the way we managed the position He gave us.

The Absent Landlord

Jesus told the parable of the absent landlord to emphasize man's accountability to God. We read in Mark 13:24, "For the Son of man is as a man taking a far journey, who left his house, and gave authority to his servants, and to every man his work, and commanded the porter to watch." The absent landlord expects his servants not only to be alert, watching for his return, but also to be actively advancing his interests. God is the absent master of the parable. He has given us talents. He has left us in charge of our lives and of His earth. One day — we know not when — He will return to demand an accounting of how we managed His property. Part of the greatness of man is that he is accountable to none other than the Lord of the Universe. Behind this accountability lies the fact of God's love. It is because we matter to Him that God cares about what we do and holds us accountable. Here lies the real basis of man's dignity and importance. Each one of us is ultimately and personally accountable to God Himself.

Reduced Accountability?

We live in a day when psychology, psychiatry and sociology are constantly trying to reduce our accountability. The truth is that we are indeed victims of many forces in life, and no one can tell just how much our own wills are responsible for what we decide to do. I don't know just how much we can blame on the anemic genes and chromosomes we inherited, or on the fouled up psychic training they foisted on us in our childhood. But I am sure of this. Somewhere within the personal dynamics of the wrong we do, somewhere inside the working of our mind or will, we make a choice for which only we can give an answer. *We* chose, we acted, and we are accountable. It's not my father, not my mother, and not my bad childhood. It's me standing in the need of forgiveness. The prodigal son in last Sunday's Gospel lesson did not blame his father for his condition. Instead, he assumed full responsibility for himself when he said, "Father, I have sinned against heaven and before you. I am not worthy to be called your son . . ." Because of this confession of personal accountability, he was gloriously and joyfully forgiven.

Videotape Playback

The reality of living one's life for Christ and being accountable to Him was brought home to me when I learned of the devices that football coaches use for training purposes. On Monday, the whole team watches a videotape of the game that was played the week before. They see everything, the good plays as well as the bad. If you ever watch one of those replays with the team members, you will realize that the players on the field are not playing the game for the audience in the grandstand but for their coach. The crowd might never know if each player has executed his specific assignment well, but the coach would know and it would be seen on the screen on Monday. We, too, have a Coach. He has given us a game plan for life. This is what the Bible is all about. He has told us that one day there will be a replay of our lives on videotape. The good plays as well as the bad will be shown. The Coach Himself will be there as Judge. In view of this, how important it is that we start playing our life to a different audience — to the Living Christ, the Great Coach, the only Judge.

Of course, no one is perfect. We are bound to have bad plays in life as well as good. On the Last Day Christ will condemn not those who have had bad plays, those who have sinned, but only those who have sinned without repenting. He will forgive and will save those who have repented. After all, isn't this why He came into the world: to seek and to save the lost? As St. Peter wrote so beautifully, "God is not willing that any should perish, but wants all to come to repentance."

11

God's Great Pleasure

On the last day it will be our Master's greatest pleasure to be able to say to those who remained faithful in their accountability to Him: "Come, O blessed of my Father. Inherit the kingdom prepared for you from the foundation of the world . . ." These beautiful words are echoed in what Matthew says earlier in his gospel, "Fear not, little flock, it is your Father's good pleasure to give you the kingdom." It will be God's greatest pleasure one day to give the kingdom to his servants who have remained faithful in their love, service and obedience to Him.

Let me leave you with just one question: The "Titanic" can happen to us at any moment. Life is fragile. It can sink at any moment through a heart attack or even an auto accident. If you were to appear before God at this moment what kind of an account would you be able to give Him for your life?

PRAYER

Grant, Lord, that we may live life in total consecration and obedience to You so that when that Day comes You may find us to be faithful servants. Amen.

GOD'S CARE PACKAGES
The Parable of the Good Samaritan.
Luke 10:25 - 39.

After WWII care packages became very well known. They contained articles of food and clothing for people in areas of desperate need and helped keep those people alive.

The term "CARE package" has taken on some new meanings in the course of time. Today a college student may refer to something he receives from home as a CARE package. It continues, however, to represent a gift from someone who cares.

The greatest CARE package in the history of the world contained a gift that St. Paul described as indescribable, ineffable, unspeakable. "Thanks to God for His unspeakable gift" he wrote.

This unspeakable gift is God's own Son. God wrapped His love in a person, the Person of His Son, Who stepped out of eternity into time and gave His life for you and me. Jesus was God's original CARE package to us!

As the gift of God came to us wrapped up in the Person of His Son, so we are called by God to become His CARE packages to the world today.

As Christians, as disciples of Jesus, we are called to become His CARE packages to a needy world.

St. Paul describes the fruit of the Spirit as "love, joy, peace, patience, kindness, goodness, faithfulness, gentleness, self-control . . ." (Gal. 5:22). None of these fruits filters down to us through the air. None grow on trees. They all come wrapped up in people.

No One Cares

Essential as it is, caring is in very short supply. A psychiatrist, Dr. Wm. Glaser, says, "At all times in our lives we must have at least one person who cares about us and whom we care

13

for ourselves. If we do not have this essential person, we will not be able to fulfill our basic needs." In order to survive, everyone needs at least one caring person and one person to care for. A man left a suicide note that said, "I have been sick for five days. No one has phoned or inquired. No one cares whether I live or die. *No one cares.*"

This is why the sin of omission is so serious. In a world so full of need, we hold back the CARE package of a kind word, a telephone call, a visit, a word of encouragement, a word of prayer, a helping hand, a listening ear, a piece of bread.

Where It All Begins

Now, being a Good Samaritan begins at home. Jesus concludes today's parable by asking "Who is your neighbor?" The answer is that "neighbor" is anyone who happens to be closest to us at the time. The priest and the levite were the people closest to the wounded man. The people who are closest to us most often use the members of our family. So, the real question is: are we Good Samaritans to the members of our family?

I would like to ask parents this question: When was the last time you said to your children, "I am proud of you. I love you. I want you to know that even though I may get busy at times and forget to tell you — I want you to know that you are a very precious person to me." If we only knew how much our children crave to hear these words from us — if we only knew! I can hear some parents objecting, "But when do my children show me any love and respect?" Well, then, maybe you need to ask yourself another question: What am I doing to earn their love and respect? How much time am I spending with them, encouraging them, listening to them, cheering them on?

Our Ticket to Heaven

True caring begins at home. Here is where being a Good Samaritan really counts. Here is where there is the greatest need for Good Samaritans. This is the real road to Jericho where most of the wounded lie. This is where we leave each other wounded by the side of the road and pass our loved ones by, totally ignoring them. Each one goes his own way. Each one does his own thing. And, as Sartre the atheist said, "hell is other people." Other people bother us. They stand in our way. They impede us. Jesus said that other people are not hell but heaven. Take the wounded man lying by the side of the road. He was really the priest's and the levite's ticket to heaven. By caring for him, they would be caring for Jesus Himself and one day Jesus would say to them, "Come, O blessed of my Father, inherit the kingdom prepared for you before the foundation of the world, for I was that wounded man lying on the side of the road and you helped me!"

Latchkey Children

Roughly 6 million mothers today have left the home to enter the work force. This means that we have substituted baby-sitters and child-care centers for 10 million latchkey children many of whom come home to nothing but a TV set. At the end of the day mom and dad come home from work physically and psychologically drained. The last thing they want is to deal with the complicated demands children rightfully make on them. The result is that we are leaving our neighbors — those closest to us — our children; we are leaving them wounded on the side of the road.

Single Parents and Quality Time

There is debate today as to whether a single parent can do a good job of raising a child. Well, I think you need not one, or two, but three parents to really do a good job: mother, father and maybe a grandparent, too! This is the kind of family support our children need.

The slogan that the social scientists invented that quality time with our children can substitute for quantity time — is full of holes. You get quality time only when you have a sufficient quantity of time. You don't suddenly say to Jimmy, "I have six minutes before my next appointment. Let's spend some quality time together." It's getting to the point now where some parents even substitute a "quality phone call" to their children.

Well, all of this — working mothers, busy fathers, baby-sitters, child-care centers, single parents, and "quality time" are wounding our children, leaving them on the side of the road, and passing them by because our priorities are not with our

15

children but with succeeding in our career, or buying a new car, or paying the mortgage, or whatever. The place where we really need Good Samaritans today is in our homes, for this is where most of our wounded are to be found.

Where It Counts Most

Let me mention one more example. There are altogether too many people today who are at their best out in the world and at their worst at home. Take this business of tone of voice. A salesman will speak in a smooth tone at work; and yet when he gets home he puts on a voice that would drive all the customers out of the store in one second flat! With outsiders we watch our words and "put up" with little things that momentarily irritate us; at home we nag each other on every little slip or defect. With outsiders we turn on the charm; at home we just don't bother. Yet where is there the greatest need for Good Samaritans today? Where but in the home to those nearest and dearest to us? If there is anything in patience, practice it at home. If there is anything in being gentle, practice it at home. If there is anything in love, practice it at home. Be God's CARE package especially to your loved ones. Don't leave them lying by the side of the road wounded.

WHO IS THIS JESUS?
Christmas.

During the Christmas rush two men were standing on Fifth Avenue at 57th Street in New York City, waiting for a red light. One of them was irritated by the traffic. "This town is totally disorganized," he growled. "Look at this traffic! It's terrible! Something ought to be done about it."

The other man was more philosophical. Thoughtfully he countered, "You know, it's astounding, the romance of it. There was a baby born of peasant parents in a little out-of-the-way place halfway around the world from here. The parents had no money or social standing, yet two thousand years later that little baby creates a traffic jam on Fifth Avenue, one of the most sophisticated streets in the world. This irritates you. Instead it should fascinate you."

If Christmas is to be more than "Ho, ho, hum, and a bottle of rum" we need to look at this Jesus.

Who is He?

Who is He Who says, "I and the Father are one" (John 10:30) and "He who has seen Me has seen the Father" (John 14:19)?

Who is this Who says that before Abraham was born, He was living: "Before Abraham was, I am" (John 8:58)?

Who is this who claims that all the Old Testament prophecies concerning the Messiah were fulfilled in Him?

Who is this of whom His enemies said, "No man ever spoke as this man"?

Who is this who assumes the awesome authority of pronouncing final judgment on humanity on the last day (Matthew 7:21 - 23)?

Who is this who equates his voice with the voice of God that spoke in the Old Testament: "You have heard that it was said to those of old, 'You shall not kill.' . . . But I say to you that everyone who is angry with his brother is liable to judgment" (Matthew 5:21 - 23)?

Who is this who said not, "I'll *show* you or *teach* you or *lead* you to the way, the truth and the life" but "I *am* the way, the truth and the life"?

Who is this who said, "I am the Alpha and the Omega, the first and the last, the beginning and the end" (Rev. 22:13)?

Who is this who stilled the storm on the Sea of Galilee, healed the sick and at whose command the dead came back to life?

Who is this of whom St. Paul said, "I can do all things through Christ who strengthens me" (Phil. 4:13)?

Who is this who said, "If you shall ask anything in my name I will do it" (John 14:14)?

Who is this who said, "Heaven and earth shall pass away, but my words shall not pass away"?

During one of our pilgrimages to the Holy Land, we were in the shepherds' fields near the cave where Jesus was born. Those were the fields where shepherds were abiding keeping their flocks by night.

One person came and he could hardly speak. He was so overcome with emotion. Yet there was a beautiful glow on his face. Pointing to Bethlehem on a hill about a mile away, he said, "What would have happened to me if Jesus had not been born over there? Life has been so wonderful, victorious, and exciting ever since I met Him."

Who is this Jesus Who changes our lives and fills them with meaning and joy?

Who is this who said, "I am the bread of life. . . . I am the light of the world. . . . I am the door. . . . I am the Good Shepherd. . . . I am the resurrection and the life"?

Who is this who said, "Come to me all you who labor and are heavy laden and I will give you rest"?

Who is this of whom St. Paul says, "That at the name of Jesus every knee shall bow . . . and every tongue confess that Jesus Christ is Lord to the glory of God the Father"?

Who is this of whom St. Paul says, "All things were created through Him and for Him" (Col. 1:16) and "in Him the whole fullness of God dwells bodily" (Col. 2:9) and "in Him all things hang together" (Col. 1:17)?

Who is this whose birth in Bethlehem of Judea changed the calendar to A.D., meaning "in the year of the Lord"? Humanity did not do this for Caesar or Napoleon, Plato or Socrates, but it did it for Jesus!

Who is He?

Well, some strange answers have been given to this question. Listen, for example, to what the Mormons say about Jesus. He is not the Second Person of the Trinity, since they reject the Christian doctrine of the Trinity. According to Mormon belief, Christ as a pre-existent spirit was the spirit brother of the devil. The blasphemy does not stop here. They go on to say that Jesus was married to both the Mary's and Martha so that he could see his seed before he was crucified. In other words Jesus was a polygamist! They also deny that Jesus was the Savior since they believe that the sacrifice of Jesus was not sufficient for the cleansing of all sin.[1] This is certainly not the Jesus we meet in the Gospels.

Who is this Jesus?

Mary Baker Eddy, founder of the Christian Scientists, produces another counterfeit Christ when she says that, "Jesus Christ is *not* God as Jesus Himself declared . . ." According to her, Jesus is not equal to God the Father. He was a great man inspired by the "Christ idea." He never really "died" at all for our sins. This is certainly not the Jesus we know in the Gospels.

Who is He — this Jesus?

The Jehovah's Witnesses not only deny that Jesus is God, they deny also his bodily resurrection; they deny that He is the Savior of the world who completely atoned for our sins. They deny heaven and hell. They deny the Trinity. According to Jehovah's Witnesses, Jesus was a creature like us — not God, not Savior, not "Light of light" not "very God of very God."

Who is He — this Jesus?

Others say that Jesus is a great moral teacher, the greatest teacher who ever lived, but *not* God. But how can He be merely a teacher and not God when He Himself *taught that He is God?* Now if you say that you believe that someone is a great teacher, you must accept what he teaches. Jesus teaches plainly that He is God. You cannot accept Him as a teacher and not accept what He taught. In other words, the option before us is

---

[1] "The Kingdom of the Cults," Walter R. Martin. Bethany Fellowship/Minneapolis, MN. 1977. p. 192.

this: Jesus is either what He says He is; God, or He is a lunatic. Any man who stands up and makes the claims Jesus made is either what He says He is or He is insane. Who is this Jesus, then? The Fathers of the early Church gave their answer quite emphatically and unequivocally: VERY GOD OF VERY GOD they said in the Nicene Creed.

Jesus Himself once asked His disciples this same question: "Who do men say that the Son of man is?" And they said, "Some say John the Baptist, others say Elijah, and others Jeremiah or one of the prophets." But Jesus was not satisfied with what others were saying about Him. He wanted the answer from them as to who He was: "But who do *you* say that I am?" He asked them. Simon Peter replied, "You are the Christ, the Son of the Living God" (Matthew 16). And Jesus blessed Peter for that answer and told him that the answer had been given to him by His Father in heaven.

Who is this Jesus? Who is He for you? We know what the Church says:

Jesus is God in the flesh. He is the eternal Word of God inviting us to fellowship with Him. He is the Good Shepherd seeking after the lost sheep — you and me — and when He finds us, He takes us into His arms and rejoices. He is the King who invites us to the Great Wedding Banquet of His Kingdom. Only the wedding to which He invites us is His marriage to us. He craves to enter into the closest and most intimate relationship with us. His desire is to come and make His home in our hearts. He has chosen to share His glory with us. He did not create us merely to be "good" people who do good things in order to attain heaven. He has created us to share His very life that we may experience His ecstatic happiness and be with Him in heaven for all eternity.

We are creatures made in His own image. To us alone of all His creation is He able to speak. He addresses us supremely through His Son Jesus, Who comes to offer us God's personalized love. He literally pursues us through the pages of the Bible and through our life on earth to give us His love.

In the words of that beautiful prayer of the liturgy: "He (God) brought us from nothingness into being. He raised us up after we had fallen into sin and death. He left nothing undone until He had lifted us up to heaven and bestowed upon us the

20

kingdom to come." He loves us and He sent Jesus not only to tell us but also to show us on the cross the height and the depth and the breadth and the width of His love. Only one thing is missing. And that is our acceptance of His love. He ecstatically waits for us to return that love. Through the Bible from the Old Testament to the New Testament, He keeps coming closer and closer to us until finally He stands just outside the door of your heart and mine and He knocks, seeking to give you the greatest of all gifts: "Behold, I stand at the door and I knock. If anyone hears my voice and opens the door, I will come in and have dinner with him and he with Me."

Who is this Jesus? Not the counterfeit Jesus of the cults but the real Jesus of the Gospels, the Jesus we preach in Church, the Jesus whose coming into the world we now celebrate. Who is He to you? Who do you say He is? Is He for you the pre-existent God become flesh? The eternal Son and Word of God? The Savior? The Prince of Peace? The Messiah? The Way? The Truth? The Life? The One Who comes to offer you God's forgiving love? The One Who comes to give you the Kingdom? The One in whose name alone we find salvation? Christ "the power of God and the wisdom of God"? Have you accepted Him as *your* Lord and God? For in Him, Jesus, God has wrapped all of His love for you. To miss out on that love is to miss the whole point of why you're here.

> Christ is born: glorify Him.
> Christ comes from heaven: go out to meet Him.
> Christ descends to earth: let us be raised on high.
> Let all the world sing to the Lord;
> Let the heavens rejoice and the earth be glad . . .
> Christ is here in the flesh:
> Let us exult with fear and joy —
> With fear, because of our sins;
> With joy, because of the hope He brings us.
> Once more the darkness is dispersed;
> Once more the light is created.
> Let the people who sat in the darkness of ignorance
> Now look upon the light of knowledge.
> The things of old have passed away;
> Behold, all things are made new . . .

The Invisible is seen;
He Whom no hand can touch is handled;
The Timeless has a beginning;
The Son of God becomes the Son of Man—
Jesus Christ, the same yesterday, today
    and for ever . . .
For the sake of my flesh He takes flesh . . .
He shares in the poverty of my flesh,
That I may share in the riches of His Godhead.

(St. Gregory of Nazianzos)

ON MAKING
LASTING INVESTMENTS
Cheesefare Sunday.
Matthew 6:14-21.

Mark Twain, the popular American humorist, achieved great fame and financial success through his writings. Yet his secret desire was to become an investor, a financier, whose well-managed money would multiply without effort. He invested in every wild scheme imaginable and lost a succession of fortunes.

Ironically, he missed the most solid investment opportunity of all. He steadfastly refused to consider investing in a new-fangled invention by Alexander Graham Bell. It was an as yet unnamed gadget that would supposedly transmit a human voice through an electric wire. Bell was short the necessary research funds and offered Twain a part interest, which he turned down. Twain never forgave himself for missing out on the greatest investment opportunity of his life: the telephone!

This brings us to the subject of investments about which we shall speak briefly this morning.

It was about investments that Jesus spoke in today's Gospel lesson when He said: "Do not lay up for yourselves treasures on earth, where moth and rust consume and where thieves break in and steal, but lay up for yourselves treasures in heaven where neither moth nor rust consumes and where thieves do not break in and steal. For where your treasure is, there will your heart be also" (Matthew 6:19-21).

It is possible — said Jesus — for people to live all their lives for treasures that will turn out to be nothing but trash.

Investing In Success

In what are we investing our life? Success? Business? Wealth? Good as these may be, can they alone satisfy our deepest hunger for meaning and fulfillment? A businessman said once, "I spent my life climbing the ladder of success — only to discover I had placed the ladder against the wrong building."

Tom Landry, head coach of the Dallas Cowboys, said once that even though he had achieved success after success in football, he felt an inexplicable emptiness in his life. This inner emptiness led him in search of the Scriptures to see if Jesus was really who He said He was. He became part of a men's Bible study group. He prayed. He made it his business to search, to investigate, to study until he found what he was looking for. He came to know for himself the meaning of what Jesus meant when He said, "I came that they may have life, and have it more abundantly." He found that all the glamour and success of football were not enough. For lasting fulfillment he needed to invest his life in Christ.

Investing In Love and Not Finding It

Some time ago, on the David Frost television show, Hugh Hefner the publisher of Playboy magazine was interviewed and asked this question: "Hugh, now that you have everything a man could possibly want — all the fame, and success, and women — what would you like now?" There was a long pause as the camera moved in on Hefner. Then he slowly replied, "David, I'd give everything I own to find . . . true love."

Hefner had everything the world could possibly offer. In fact, he had invested his life in what our society calls "love," but in the end he had not found true love. How can anyone without God?

Investments Without God

The writer of "Ecclesiastes" expressed well what happens to people who invest in everything but God. Listen:

"I tried cheering myself with wine and embracing folly. I wanted to see what was worthwhile for men to do under heaven the few days of their lives. I undertook great projects, I built houses for myself and planted vineyards. I made gardens and parks and planted all kinds of fruit in them. I owned more heads and flocks than anyone in Jerusalem before me. I

amassed silver and gold for myself, and the treasure of kings and provinces. I became greater by far than anyone in Jerusalem before me. I denied myself nothing my eyes desired; I refused my heart no pleasure. Yet when I surveyed all that my hands had done and what I had toiled to achieve, everything was meaningless, a chasing after wind; nothing was gained under the sun" (Ecclesiastes).

Investing In Worship

There was a man once who attended the liturgy every Sunday but not because he wanted to do so. He went just to please his wife. He never participated in the liturgy. He was there only in body. He never really listened to God's word when it was read or preached. He never prayed the prayers with the priest and never received Jesus in the Sacrament of Communion. He put nothing into the worship service and got nothing from it. Then suddenly all of that changed. One day he became aware of the presence of God in the liturgy, and his whole outlook was transformed. From that time on, he invested his whole self into worship, and was amazed as what he got out of it.

God will not come alive to you unless you invest yourself in Him.

Many Kinds of Investments

There are many kinds of investments.

For example, there was a family in Colorado that tried unsuccessfully for years to save enough money to replace their ancient bathroom fixtures with new modern ones. But each year as skiing time rolled around, it seemed the bathroom money went for a family skiing trip.

The children are now grown. One of the sons recently wrote home to the parents. He talked about the annual skiing trips, the good times they had had together, and how much he enjoyed them and how often he thought about them.

His father said, "I can't imagine my son writing and saying, 'Dad, I sure remember our swell bathroom fixtures.'"

25

The parents had chosen to invest in family togetherness — and it paid rich dividends. The finest investment parents can make is to provide a home where God is real and where parents and children come to Jesus every day in prayer. An investment in family togetherness and worship pays the richest dividends.

An Investment In God's Word

John Wanamaker, an outstanding merchant of the 19th century, began his career as an errand boy at $1.25 a week and later became one of America's leading businessmen. When asked what he considered to be the best investment he had ever made, he replied, "I have, of course, made large purchases of property in my lifetime, involving millions of dollars. But when I was only 11 years old, I made my biggest purchase of all. From my teacher in a little mission Sunday school, I bought a small red leather Bible. It cost me $2.75. I paid for it in small installments from my own money that I had earned."

The Bible was Wanamaker's greatest investment because its priceless truths brought spiritual vitality to his life and gave him strength of character. By reading and believing in God's Word he not only established a solid foundation for his life, but he was also guided by God in everything he did.

To invest part of one's time daily in reading God's Word, in seeking His guidance and wisdom is an investment of incalculable value.

An Investment In Teaching

A man in his fifties was dying. He said to his pastor who was by his bedside, "Pastor, ten years ago the church asked me to teach a class of nine-year-old boys in Sunday school. I told them I was too busy. And I was. I was in the prime of my life and rapidly rising in business affairs. And now, ten years later, here I am, dying, with the greatest regret of my life being that I did not accept that responsibility. If ten years ago, I had taken time to teach that class of ten boys, by now perhaps 100 boys would have passed through my hands. I would have invested my life in the lives of 100 boys, and many of them would be scattered throughout the world growing in service and usefulness as Christian young men. I would have made an investment

26

in time and eternity through them. But now I must go empty-handed before my Master. I cannot take any of my money or business with me."

It is terrible to come to the end of one's life with such regret for not having made a lasting investment.

An Investment You Can Keep

When a father invests in his son's education, it is an investment that outlasts the father's life. It extends at least to the time of the son's death, and perhaps beyond that, in the grandchildren as well as in the people whose lives the son touches and blesses through his education.

But Jesus, Who is the greatest and the best investment counselor in the universe, talks about investments that produce dividends not for one or two generations but eternally. We often hear people say, "You can't take it with you!" But Jesus says, "You *can* keep wealth, and you *can* take it with you by sending it on ahead."

Jesus talks about two kinds of investments: (1) *investments on earth* "where moth and rust consume and where thieves break in and steal," and (2) *investments in heaven:* "Where neither moth nor rust consume and where thieves do not break in and steal." And He tells us to be careful about *where* we invest our wealth because "where your treasure is, there will your heart be also." We can put our heart in the right place — said Jesus — by placing our wealth in the right place because our heart will always be where our wealth is.

Like Mark Twain, it is possible to make many investments in life, and to miss out on the greatest investment of all. It is possible to live all our life for treasures that will turn out to be trash. But it doesn't have to be. Jesus challenges us to invest in eternal treasures.

How Long Will They Last?

One thing we need to ask about the investments we make in life is: how long will they last? There are some good things in life in which people invest. There are even some great things, but they are not the greatest. They are not the greatest because they are temporary. One day they will pass away. All that is in the world, the lust of the eye, the lust of the flesh, and the pride of life are but for a little while. Love not the world, therefore, or the things of the world. And don't invest your all in the world. Nothing the world contains is worth what your soul is worth. "What shall it profit a man if he gain the whole world and lose his soul?" asked Jesus. The immortal soul must give itself to Someone Who is immortal. Let our greatest investment, therefore, be in the Eternal God and His kingdom; the one thing that will outlast all others; the one coinage that will be current in the universe when all other coinages shall be useless.

God Has Invested In Us

God has invested Himself in each one of us. We are His greatest investment. He owns us not only because He created us but also because He paid a price for us. He bought and redeemed us, not with silver or gold, but with the precious blood of His only Son. "You are not your own. You were bought with a price. So glorify God in your body," says St. Paul. So the Lord has a right to say, "What you are and what you have are mine. Everything is from Me and for Me. Let Me tell you how to use it while you manage it for Me for a few years as my stewards. I gave it to you because I invest in people. I love people and I want them to be with Me in eternal glory. I want *you* to invest in people and to make a holy use of your possessions."

Invest In Christ and His People

It is not money itself but the love of money that prevents people from making lasting investments. You can live for money even without having much of it. You can live for it when you think of it as the only thing worth living for. Place Christ first in your life and your money will be translated into love and compassion as it feeds the hungry, enriches the poor, clothes the naked—in the name of Christ and for the love of Christ.

Who says you can't take it with you? Not Jesus! Listen to John the Evangelist writing in the 14th chapter of Revelation:

"Then I heard a voice from heaven saying, write this: Happy are the dead who die in the Lord from now on. Certainly so, answers the Spirit. They will enjoy rest from their hard work, for *they take with them the results of their service."*

We can take our treasures with us by sending them on ahead. When we invest our life in lifting the fallen, in visiting the tired and discouraged, in feeding the hungry, in clothing the naked, we become the wise investors God wants us to be. Whatever we invest in the direction of Christ and His kingdom will never deflate. It will never be taken away from us. The interest will keep growing eternally.

"I will not just give my life. . . . I will not just spend my life. . . . I will invest my life," said Helen Keller.

I conclude with the words of St. Paul who had himself made the greatest investment of all, investing his life totally and completely in Christ:

"All those things that I might count as profit, I now reckon as loss for Christ's sake . . . as complete loss for the sake of what is so much more valuable, the knowledge of Christ Jesus my Lord. For His sake I have thrown everything away. I consider it all as mere garbage, so that I might gain Christ and be completely united with Him."

PRAYER

Heavenly Father, as You invested Your Precious Son in us and gave us the unsearchable riches of the kingdom, may we invest all we are and have in loving and serving You and Your suffering children here on earth. Amen.

COME AND SEE

First Sunday of Lent.
John 1:44 - 52.

After he had met Jesus, Philip — the apostle — found Nathanael and said, "We have found Him! We have found Him of Whom Moses . . . and the prophets wrote, Jesus of Nazareth, the son of Joseph." But Nathanael said, "Can anything good come out of Nazareth?" Philip's reply was quick, "Come and see."

We shall concentrate briefly on those two words: *"Come* and *see."*

Jesus has always been telling us to come and see. When Thomas said that he would not believe because he had not seen the resurrected Christ, Jesus appeared to him and invited him to come and see and even touch His wounds. Thomas came and saw and touched and believed. He was never the same again.

When Peter confessed that Jesus was the Messiah, the Son of the Living God, Jesus charged him not to reveal publicly the mystery of who He was. He wanted people to believe in Him not because they heard it second-hand from others. He wanted people to come to Him personally, first-hand, to see Him, listen to Him, follow Him, and discover by an intensely personal experience who He is. Many of us have a faith, but it is a second-hand faith that we have inherited from our families. We need to make it a first-hand, personal faith of our own, like Job's faith when he said, "I had learned of You (O Lord) by the hearing of the ear; but now I see You with my own eyes." This can happen only if we come to Jesus personally, commit our life to Him, and see for ourselves what miracles He can work in our lives, what understanding He can give us, what power, what love, what grace, what forgiveness, what peace, what joy!

"Come and *see."* Come and see what a change Jesus can effect in life. He will destroy the old, sinful nature to allow the image of God in us to shine forth in all its attractive splendor.

31

He will help us achieve our great potential of becoming "partakers of divine nature." He will take away our guilt. He will help carry our burdens. He will raise us when we fall. He will comfort us in our affliction. He will strengthen us in our weakness.

"Come and *see."* Come and see how He can change your tastes in life. A modestly paid newspaper reporter turned to magazine writing and became an immediate success. With a soaring income, her mode of living changed radically. No more scrimping, she spent on a lavish scale. Then came the stock market crash. Her investments evaporated. Even worse, her spirits hit bottom.

Friends tried to get her to rebound, but she did not respond. "Come, now, snap out of it," said a friend. "You were poor before and it wasn't so awful."

"But it was different then," moaned the writer. "Now I have expensive tastes."

After we come to Christ, our sense of taste improves so drastically that we can never be satisfied any more with the cheap and the sordid—not after we have tasted the finest! "Taste and see that the Lord is good."

"Come and *see."* Come and see what great things God can do in your life. Come and see what purpose and meaning He can add to your life. Come and see what a great plan He has for your life. Come and see what love you will find in Him. Come and see the promises He has made to you. Come and see what a great victory He has won for you through His death and resurrection. Come and see how eager He is to give you the kingdom. Come and see what a great future He has prepared for you. Come and open the door to let Him come into your heart. He wants to have dinner with you as He did with Zacchaeus. He wants to establish a close, personal, intimate relationship with you.

"Come and *see."*

Huxley, the great agnostic, one day approached a farmer who had a simple and radiant Christian faith. "Tell me what your Christian faith means to you and why you are a Christian," asked Huxley. The farmer refused saying, "You could demolish my arguments in an instant. I'm not clever enough to argue with you." Huxley said gently, "I don't want to argue with you; I

just want you to tell me simply what this Christ means to you."
The farmer did. When he had finished, there were tears in the
great agnostic's eyes. "I would give my right hand," he said,
"if only I could believe that." It was no clever argument that
touched Huxley's heart, just the personal religious experience of
a simple farmer who came to Jesus and saw. "Can anything
good come out of Nazareth? Come and see. . . . Taste and see
that the Lord is good."

A Scientist's Confession

A brilliant scientist said once,
"Before my lecture I want to tell you something. I am a
Christian. I was brought up in a Christian home with my
brother, and the two of us were the closest pals. We were both
at the university together. My father and mother were deeply
religious. My brother and I had no time for religion. We thought
that religion was all right for old people, but we were scientists
and we thought we had found our way through by what we were
pleased to call scientific methods. Then my brother was killed.
My father and mother had resources, and with their resources
they could meet that shattering loss. But I had no one. I had no
resources at all. One night, broken-hearted and with all my
proud science in ruined uselessness at my feet, I knelt down. I
did not know how to pray. I had scorned prayer, but I put out
my hand and I found it was grasped. I knew that Someone was
coming to my help and somehow I knew it was Christ. I have
been a Christian ever since and no one, nothing, will ever take
Christ away from me any more."
But don't take someone else's word for it.
"Come and see" for yourself.
"Taste and see that the Lord is good."

PRAYER

Thank You, Lord, for this beautiful invitation.
Help each one of us to come and discover personally what great things You have in store for those
who come to You with broken and contrite hearts.
Amen.

"RISE AND GET RID OF YOUR STRETCHER"

Second Sunday of Lent.
Mark 2:1-12.

A pastor tells of an elderly lady who came to his office one day. He noticed that her right arm was paralyzed.

"Do you think I can ever be forgiven?" she asked. Slowly, she began to unravel the whole story.

During the First World War she was married, and six days later she saw her young husband sail for the battlefields of France.

Being desperately lonely, she formed a relationship with another man soon after her husband left, hiding it from him. Letters went to and fro from France for some months, then came the news that her husband had been killed in action.

Later, she married the one with whom she had been living. After forty years of marriage, he died. Now she was sick and old and tired. She found herself thinking remorsefully of that first soldier husband. For her unfaithfulness, though he had known nothing about it, she now was overwhelmed with guilt.

Recently her right arm had become paralyzed. "The doctor tells me he can find nothing wrong with it. However, there is no strength in it. I cannot use my arm or hand," she said.

Then, shyly she turned back the lapel of her coat, revealing the ribbons and decorations sent to her following her first husband's death. "Do you think God could ever forgive me for what I did to him?" she asked tearfully.

The pastor tried to assure her of God's forgiving love when we repent. "It is for people just like you," he said, "that Jesus came and died on the cross as our Savior." Then he pronounced God's forgiveness: "Your sins are forgiven," he said to her, "go in peace."

Some weeks later, she came to see the pastor again. Walking toward him confidently and, extending her hand for a clasp, she said to him, "Look, my arm is healed."

Jesus knew all about the power that guilt has to paralyze a person's body and spirit.

The Paralytic

In the Gospel lesson today a group of four friends brought a paralyzed man to Jesus on a stretcher. At once Jesus knew that this man's paralysis was due to sin, so He said to him, "Your sins are forgiven."

Having forgiven the sick man's sins, Jesus proceeded from the cause (sin) to the effect (paralysis). He then said to the forgiven paralytic: "Take up your stretcher and walk." And the paralyzed man walked!

Guilt! How many today are paralyzed because of unforgiven sin? They cover it up. They let it fester within. Like the paralytic, they know they are sinners, at least in a vague sort of way. But unlike the paralytic they lack his will to be cured, to be forgiven. They do not seek the forgiveness that offers a new way of life; instead they seek to punish themselves for their sins. This is why they hang on to the stretcher — the symbol of self-punishment — as if the suffering of the stretcher can atone for their sins. As long as they are suffering they feel they are paying for their sins. It lessens the agony for them. It's not the stretcher, however, but the Cross that atones and cleanses. Not all the world's stretchers or suffering can wipe away our sins. Only the Savior, only the Redeemer, only Jesus can do that.

The Great Desire

Here is where many of us differ from the paralytic. He *wanted* to be cured, to be forgiven, as much as his friends wanted him cured, not only because they tore through a roof to get him to Jesus but also because when Jesus said, "Your sins are forgiven," the paralytic believed Jesus immediately. When Jesus asked him to stand up, he did not argue with Him as to whether or not he had been really healed. He believed. He rose to his feet.

The Great Faith

The healing came about not only because of the great desire to be forgiven but also because of their great faith. The Gospel says, "When Jesus *saw their faith."* Whose faith? The faith of the four or the faith of the five? I believe the faith of the paralytic is included. When Jesus sees faith even today, He responds with forgiveness, healing and peace.

"Teknon"

So, come to Jesus! Don't be afraid of Him. When Jesus spoke to the paralyzed man, He used the word *teknon* which in Greek means "my little child." Jesus spoke tenderly to the paralytic — as tenderly as He would have spoken to a child. And so He will speak to you!

As Jesus said to the paralytic, so He can say to you today, "Your sins are forgiven" (Mark 2:5). No other person has the authority to say this to you — only Jesus. And when we hear these liberating words from Jesus, the world's heaviest burden will fall from our shoulders, the peace of God will pervade our being, and our heart will sing for joy.

"My son, my daughter, your sins are forgiven." The next words are "Rise and take up your stretcher . . ." Get off that stretcher of paralysis, the stretcher of self-punishment, the stretcher of self-pity, the stretcher of inactivity. Throw it away and go, become like those four friends who carried you to Jesus. Bringing someone to Jesus is the greatest thing one friend can do for another. In liberating us from the paralysis of sin and guilt, Jesus makes us *responsible* members of His Body, the Church, like those four friends who symbolize so beautifully what every member of the Church should be doing: bringing others to Jesus! The word *responsible* by the way, comes from two words: *response* and *able*. In healing us and making us whole, Jesus makes us responsible, i.e., *able* to *respond* to His will, to love, to bear one another's burdens, to serve one another in love, to be like those four friends.

I Am The Paralytic

A Lutheran pastor tells of being struck by a huge wave while surfing in California. His body was dashed against the beach with such great force that his neck was broken and he lay there helpless, unable to move a single muscle in his body, completely paralyzed.

As he was being rushed to the hospital in an ambulance, he said he thought of the paralytic in today's Gospel lesson on which he had preached so often. And he thought of the four men who brought him to Jesus on a stretcher.

Only now — he said — he was the paralytic, completely helpless and totally dependent on the doctors and nurses without whose help he was a dead man. He thought of them as the four friends who stopped at nothing to bring help to the helpless one.

He applied this to the Church and discovered the importance of the Church as the caring family of God's people. That's how we, the members of Christ's Body — the Church, should care for others. As the members of the hospital staff cared for him; as the four friends cared enough for the paralytic to raze a roof in order to bring him to Jesus; as Jesus Himself cared for us in healing us, forgiving us, loving us, feeding us, washing our feet, and bleeding for us on the Cross, so we are called to care and love and serve and bear one another's burdens.

How many paralytics do we know today who might be healed through our help? People paralyzed by fear, guilt, discouragement, weakness or frustration. People unable to realize their God-given potential for want of appreciation, affection, encouragement, recognition. People whose minds and spirits have become warped and twisted under their many burdens.

So Jesus says to us today: "Now that your sins have been forgiven, get rid of the stretcher of immobility and inactivity. Be responsible. Go out and become like those four friends to the many other paralytics that lie on your doorstep. Bring them to Me for forgiveness and healing."

PRAYER

Grant me, dear Lord, the compunction to repent of my sins this Lent, to seek your forgiveness, to throw away the stretcher of self-punishment, the stretcher of excuse upon excuse, to rise to the new life, the new potential to which You are calling me in Christ Jesus my Lord. Amen.

THE KINGDOM OF GOD COME WITH POWER

Third Sunday of Lent.
Mark 8:34 - 9:1.

Jesus said, "Truly I say to you, there are some standing here who will not taste death before they see the kingdom of God come with power" (Mark 9:1).

Some thought that when Jesus spoke these words "the kingdom of God come with power" He was referring to His Second Coming. But He was not. Those who "would not taste death," i.e., would not die before seeing "the kingdom of God come with power" did indeed see this on the day of Pentecost. For this is when the Holy Spirit came *in power* to establish the kingdom. Jesus had promised His disciples after the Resurrection: "But you will receive power after the Holy Spirit has come upon you . . ." (Acts 1:8). When the Holy Spirit came upon the apostles on Pentecost, they experienced a power they never dreamed possible; a power that sent them to the far corners of the earth to be witnesses for Christ; a power that gave Peter, who had denied Jesus three times, the fearlessness to stand up courageously and say to the Roman authorities who sought to prevent him from preaching: "It is better to obey God rather than man;" a power which enabled the early Christians to sing hymns of praise to God as the lions charged at them in the Roman arena; a power that enabled Stephen, the first martyr, to pray for those who were stoning him to death, "Father, do not lay this sin against them" (Acts 7:60); a power that made Paul and Silas sing at midnight while chained in a prison dungeon where they were being held for preaching Christ.

How Does It Become A Reality?

Where is this power today? How do we receive it? How can we not taste death before we experience the kingdom of God come with power?

39

First, how does the kingdom of God come with power become reality for us? It happens when we open the door to receive Christ into our hearts. As Jesus said "Behold, I stand at the door and knock. If anyone hears my voice and opens the door I will come in to him and have dinner with him and he with Me." Our God is not an absent God. He is a God constantly present to us. In fact, He stands just outside the door of your heart and mine seeking to enter to empower us for the tasks of life. When we open the door to let Jesus enter — and we do this through prayer each day, through repentance, through obedience, through the Sacrament of His Presence — Holy Communion, and through His word in the Holy Scriptures — when we open the door for Jesus to enter our lives, He does not come alone. He brings with Him the Father's love and the power of the Holy Spirit. I love the illustration St. Irenaios uses. He says that when we open the door to receive Jesus, He will come to us with His two arms stretched out to us. The one arm represents God the Father; the other arm the Holy Spirit. When we approach Him, He will place those two arms around us in an embrace of love as He breathes upon us the Spirit of power. We shall leave that embrace supercharged with God's love and power. This is how the kingdom of God comes with power today. Through prayer we can open the door to Jesus each day to experience the empowering embrace of God's love.

Two Keys

Someone once said that man's heart is like a garden, a secret garden which God has kept uniquely for Himself. That garden is locked like a safe deposit box. It has two keys as does every safe deposit box. God has one key. Man has the other key. Hence not even God can get in without man's consent. God's key — the key of His love and power — is already in the lock. Man's key — which is our free will — is not yet in the lock. God is waiting for us to insert our key to open the box — the greatest treasure box in the universe — the box, or rather the Person, in Whom all "treasures of wisdom and knowledge are hid," Christ "the power of God and the wisdom of God."

40

Has "the kingdom of God come with power" for you? Do you open the door of your soul daily through prayer to receive Christ's love and power? Are you living a defeated life or a victorious life? Are you living *under* your circumstances or *above* the circumstances of your life? There is power just a prayer away from you! Although just a weak earthen vessel, the body was created to house a great treasure. "We have this treasure in earthen vessels . . ." wrote St. Paul. This treasure is God's kingdom come with power within each of us. "The kingdom of God is within you," said Jesus.

Created To Be
Armories of His Power

What a tragedy it would be if we would build a church to worship the living God and have our children use it to store grain. What a far greater tragedy it is when God creates us to be the dwelling place of His Spirit and kingdom, and we turn ourselves into mere containers for good food on the inside, and surfaces for cosmetics and fabrics on the outside. We were not created to be receptacles for food or mannequins for the display of exquisite dresses and expensive suits. We were created to be temples of God's Spirit, chalices of His presence, armories of His power, fortresses of His strength.

Has the kingdom of God come with power for you? It can, if you hear His voice and open the door to Jesus.

A Testimony of Power

Listen to this testimony from a person for whom the kingdom of God had indeed come with power. He says,

> *"Christ is that in me which holds me steady and calm in the midst of confusion. Christ is that in me which undergirds my efforts and strengthens my will. Christ is that in me which says, 'Keep on. Take one step more.' Christ is that in me which speaks through me in words that convey feelings of peace, trust, and understanding. Christ is that in me which banishes fear. Christ is that in me which rises triumphant out of every trial. Christ is that in*

me which never accepts defeat. I can do all things through Christ Who strengthens me."

What Christ Brings With Him

If I were to ask you the question: "What does Jesus bring with Him when we open the door and let Him come into our lives?" what would you answer? Well, here are some of the treasures He brings:

1. "The kingdom of God come with power;" He brings that!
2. Forgiveness of sins; He brings that!
3. Inward cleansing; He brings that!
4. Peace with God; He brings that!
5. Eternal life, He brings that!
6. The gift of the Holy Spirit, He brings that!
7. Love,
8. Joy,
9. Victory over temptation,
10. Resurrection from the dead,
11. A glorified body,
12. Immortality,
13. A dwelling place in the house of the Lord forever.

If the kingdom of God has come with power for you, then you have received, are receiving, and one day will receive in full all these blessings and more.

The Great Question

The most important question in life is this: on which side of the door of your life is Jesus? Is He inside or outside? We are not really living until we open the door to Him. To open the door to Jesus is to experience the kingdom of God come with power. To close the door on Him is death. As the Apostle John writes, "He who believes in the Son has eternal life; he who does not obey the Son shall not see life . . ." (John 3:36).

When we open the door through faith, prayer and Communion, He enters. What happens when He enters? Does He find our soul blackened with sin? He makes it whiter than snow. Does He find us naked? He clothes us with the royal robes of a prince or princess. Does He find us thirsty and starving? He places us before the Messianic banquet table overflowing with manna from heaven. Does He find us living in a filthy hovel? He transforms the hovel into a sacred temple. "Do you not know that you are temples of the Holy Spirit and that God's Spirit dwells in you?" (St. Paul).

This is what happens to you when you open the door to let Jesus in. The kingdom of God comes to you with power.

PRAYER

Come, Lord Jesus, You are just what I need. Make Your kingdom come in me. Rule over me as my King and Lord. Govern my life. Make me obedient to Your will. Let Your Holy Spirit come to fill me with Your power, to overcome my many weaknesses, to enable me to live not under *but* above *my circumstances. For You alone are able to do exceeding abundantly above all that we ask or think. Amen.*

WHY SUFFERING?
Fourth Sunday of Lent.
Mark 9:17-31.

And they brought the boy to Him; and when the spirit saw him, immediately it convulsed the boy, and he fell on the ground and rolled about, foaming at the mouth. And Jesus asked his father; "How long has he had this?" And he said, "From childhood. And it has often cast him into the fire and into the water, to destroy him; but if you can do anything, have pity on us and help us." And Jesus said to him, "If you can! All things are possible to him who believes." Immediately the father of the child cried out and said, "I believe; help my unbelief!"

One reason for the father's unbelief no doubt was the condition of his son. Here was a boy who could not play as other boys could. If he were left alone in the home, he was liable to fall in the fire. He could not look forward to a normal manhood. He could not marry and have a home; it would even be hard for him to make a living. Yet the boy had done no wrong. He was completely innocent.

This father had been told that God made us and that God was good. But if that be true, then how could you explain why a good God would make a child so afflicted? Why would God allow him to suffer all of his life when the child had done nothing to deserve it?

A Great Problem

Here we have an even greater problem. Not only do we become concerned about belief in God, but also in the character of God. Better to have no God, if He is a bad God. But if we claim a creator God who is good, how do we explain all the evil in the world? If I slipped in at night and set your house on fire, I would be convicted of crime. Yet again and again bolts of lightning come from the sky and burn up people's homes. If I set off a dynamite charge under your house and kill you, it would be murder. Yet the earthquake comes and kills people wholesale. The problem of evil is one reason why it is hard to believe. "Lord, I believe; help my unbelief."

But if, because of evil, we decide not to believe in God, then we have before us an even greater problem. How are we to explain the goodness in the world? For example, one can go to Calvary, and if he centers his attention on the cross with all of its pain and suffering, he might conclude there is no God. One of the thieves who died by Jesus' side did just that. "If you are the Christ," he said, "come down from the cross and we will believe." It was really a sneer, an expression of unbelief.

Fix Your Attention on Jesus

But the thief crucified on the other side of Christ fixed his attention not on the cross, but on the Christ. As he saw Him, he began to believe, and said, "Remember me, Lord." And Jesus said to him, "Today you will be with me in heaven."

If we are to find the answer to evil, we, too, must look to Jesus on the cross Who overcame evil once and for all, and Who today helps us use the evil that befalls us for good.

"All things work together for good," said Paul. But he did not stop there. He never suggested that all things work together for good unconditionally and automatically. "All things work together for good *to those who love God.*" There is the key! It depends on our faith, on our love, on our attitude, on our response. God gives us the grace to use suffering creatively. "I do not want to die," wrote Katherine Mansfield near the end, "without leaving a record of my belief that suffering can be overcome. For I do believe it. Everything in life that we really accept undergoes a change. So suffering becomes love."

For the Christian, no experience in life, bad or good, is ever wasted. God can take anything that happens to us and use it for our good if we love Him and cooperate with His will.

A School - Not An Amusement Park

The world is not an amusement park where pleasure is the chief end of man. It is a school where the chief end of man is holiness, growth into the image and likeness of God. God uses our suffering to make us into the people He wants us to be.

No wonder the writer to the Hebrews said, "God disciplines us for our own good, that we may share in His holiness. No discipline seems pleasant at the time, but painful. Later on, however, it *produces* a harvest of righteousness and peace for those who have been trained by it" (Hebrews 12:10,11).

In a very real sense, suffering actualizes our hope — our hope of sharing the glory of God. "The doom of our greatness," to quote P. T. Forsyth, "is that God wants us to be like Jesus Christ. We will not only be with Him in His glory — understanding, appreciating all that is true about Him — but we ourselves are 'being transformed into His likeness with ever-increasing glory, which comes from the Lord, who is the Spirit'" (II Corinthians 3:18).

God uses our suffering to rub off sharp corners, to refine our temperaments, to loosen our hold on what is unworthy, to teach us to rely on Him alone. Suffering is indeed the proving ground of faith. It is a badge of admission into the kingdom. "Through much tribulation we must enter the Kingdom of God," says the Bible.

An Eternal Weight of Glory

"This slight momentary affliction is preparing for us an eternal weight of glory beyond all comparison, because we look not to the things that are seen but to the things that are unseen; for the things that are seen are transient, but the things that are unseen are eternal" (II Corinthians 4:17 - 18). Our affliction, says Paul, is *slight* and *momentary* compared to the *eternal weight of glory* it is preparing for us. "Beyond all comparison," he says. The glory that results far exceeds any suffering we may endure on earth. "If we suffer with him, we shall also reign with him," he says. Our present sufferings will not last forever; the day will come when they will be forgotten. But the glory they produce will last and last forever and ever.

When the violinist tightens the strings of a violin, he does not do it to torture them, but to bring out music better than before.

"More than that, we rejoice in our sufferings, knowing that suffering produces endurance, and endurance produces character, and character produces hope, and hope does not disappoint

47

us, because God's love has been poured in our hearts through the Holy Spirit which has been given to us" (Romans 5:3 - 5).

God Will Be Perfecting Us

There are those who say that if only we had enough faith, God would heal all our diseases and there would be no more suffering. These people need to take a much closer look at God's word. "When I am weak, then I am strong" (II Corinthians 12:10). "My grace is made perfect in weakness" (St. Paul). It is when the kingdom of God will be established in all its fullness that there will be no more suffering, no more pain, no more death. Until then, God will be perfecting us.

"I have known," said Ralph Erskine, lying racked with pain, "more of God since I came to this bed of pain than through all my life."

"The darkness," exclaimed Kagawa of Japan, describing what it felt like when he thought he was going blind, "the darkness is a holy of holies of which no one can rob me. In the darkness I meet God face to face."

And here is this amazing statement that we find in Hebrews, surely one of the most daring summaries of the life of Jesus ever penned: "Son though He (Jesus) was, yet He learned by all He suffered!" In Hebrews 2:10 we read that God made Jesus "perfect through suffering." The great spiritual writer, George Macdonald, wrote, "The Son of God suffered unto the death, not that men might not suffer, but that their sufferings might be like His." Redemptive!

Great Saints - Great Sufferers!

The problem of evil is raised far more often by the spectators of life than by the actual combatants. You will hardly ever find that the great sufferers are the great skeptics. Quite the reverse. It is the spectators — the people who are outside, looking on at the tragedy — from whose ranks the skeptics come. It is not those who are actually in the arena, and who know suffering from the inside. Indeed, the fact is that it is the world's greatest sufferers who have produced the most shining examples of unconquerable faith.

Who are the men and women whose names stand on the dramatic roll-call of the faithful in *Hebrews?* Are they men and women whose days were happy, unclouded, and serene; souls for whom the sun was always shining and the skies unvisited by cloud or storm? If anyone imagines that such is the background of faith, let him listen to this—"They were stoned, they were sawn in two, were tempted, were slain with the sword, destitute, afflicted, tormented; they wandered in deserts, and in mountains, and in dens and caves of the earth." These are the saints of the Bible. It is not from sheltered ways and quiet, sequestered paths, but from a thousand crosses, that the cry ascends—"Hallelujah! For the Lord God omnipotent reigns."

"We learn only through suffering," said Aeschylus. "God instructs the heart, not by ideas, but by pains and contradictions," said Jean Pierre de Caussade. Strength is born in the deep silence of long-suffering hearts, not amid joy. C. S. Lewis said once, "God whispers to us in our pleasures, speaks to us in our consciences but shouts in our pains: it is His megaphone to rouse a deaf world."

Bitter But Not Bad

An ancient rabbi said, "When a man suffers, he ought not to say: 'That's bad! That's bad!' Nothing that God imposes on man is bad. But it is alright to say: 'That's bitter!' For among medicines there are some that are made with bitter herbs." To those who love God, suffering may be bitter but not bad.

Rejoice that God loves us that much. Be glad that He wants us to be a little breathless for heaven. Be thankful that He never wastes any of our experiences.

"Don't be surprised, dear friends, at the painful trials you are suffering, as though something strange were happening to you. But rejoice that you participate in Christ's suffering, so that you may be overjoyed when His glory is revealed." So wrote St. Peter to first-century Christians (I Peter 4:12, 13), and it applies to us today.

Not An Explanation But A Victory

Man's main concern with the dark fact of suffering is not to find an explanation: it is to find power to overcome and victory.

49

And that is what God gives us in Christ. He gives us the grace to turn our scars into stars.

"In all these things," wrote St. Paul who had tested the promise of God to the hilt in the worst tragedies of life, and therefore had a right to speak, "in all these things" — these horrible things which happen to us, these physical pains, these mental agonies, these spiritual midnights of the soul — "we are more than conquerors," not through our own strength or bravery, not through our own stamina or perseverance, but "through Him Who loved us" — through the power of God in Christ Jesus.

That is the only answer to the mystery of suffering; and the answer is a question: Will you let God into your life to let Him reign as King? Will you surrender your pain, your brokenness to Jesus? That is when God can take crushed flowers and produce perfume.

Don't Throw Me On the Scrap Heap

A blacksmith who had a profound faith in Jesus was asked one day by one of his friends, "Why do you have so much trouble? I have watched you since you became a Christian and you have had many problems. I thought that when a person gave himself to God his troubles were over." A smile came across the blacksmith's face as he replied, "Do you see this piece of steel? I'm going to use it for the springs of a carriage. But first it needs to be heated. Then I hammer it, bend it, and shape it the way I want it. Sometimes, however, I find that the steel is too brittle to be used, so I have to throw it on the scrap heap. As scrap, the steel is worth just a few pennies, but as a carriage spring, it is very valuable. Ever since I began applying this idea to my life, I have been saying to God, 'Lord, test me in any way You choose, but don't throw me on the scrap heap.'"

SHALL I TAKE AWAY PAIN?

The cry of man's anguish went up to God:
  "Lord take away pain —
The Shadow that darkens the world Thou hast made,
  The close-coiling chain

50

That strangles the heart; the burden that weighs
    On the wings that would soar.
Lord, take away pain from the world Thou hast made,
    That it love Thee more."

Then answered the Lord to the cry of His world:
    "Shall I take away pain
And with it the power of the soul to endure,
    Made strong by the strain?
Shall I take away pity that knits heart to heart,
    And sacrifice high?
Will you lose all your heroes that lift from the fire
    White brows to the sky?
Shall I take away love, that redeems with a price
    And smiles at its loss?
Can ye spare from your lives, that would climb unto me,
    The Christ on His cross?"

THE SIN
THAT CRUCIFIED JESUS

Fifth Sunday of Lent.
Mark 10:32-45.

Someone once asked a clerk at a large department store, "What do you have for the man who has everything?" The clerk replied, "Envy. Nothing but envy."

Envy and jealousy are identical twins. They walk hand in hand through our lives. Like the sins of pride and anger, envy is an all-too-common sin. Few of us escape its clutches. "I don't have a jealous bone in my body" is more talk than reality.

The subject of envy is brought up in the Gospel lesson today. The ten disciples were envious of James and John when the two requested of Jesus that they be first in the kingdom.

Even the great saints had to deal with envy. There is a powerful legend told about Moses who led God's people through the wilderness for forty years. One day he pled with God that he be allowed to live long enough to see the Promised Land. God replied that He had ordained that Joshua succeed him and take leadership. Moses said, "That's O.K., God, I'll be glad to be Joshua's servant. Just let me live long enough to see the Land before I die." God said "O.K." The day came when the cloud, representing God's presence, appeared. Instead of Moses, Joshua, the new leader, now walked into the cloud to consult with God. Moses, who had been doing this for forty years, had to stay outside. He felt so disheartened as a result, that he called God and said to Him, "O.K., God. Now I'm ready to go. Take me." He felt he was becoming so envious that it was preferable to die than to live in envy.

We note in the Scriptures that the Apostle Peter was envi-ous of the Apostle John, who was young and smart and special to Jesus. One day when Jesus told Peter how he would die, Peter pointed to John and said, "Lord, what about him?" The Lord gave Peter some quick and helpful advice. He told him,

"Peter, you've got only two things to do. Number one, mind your own business, and number two, follow me" (John 21:21, 22). This is pretty good advice for envy which is always concerned about other people and their business.

Joseph was a boy of splendid character, yet remember how his envious brothers hated him! Abel was accepted of God, but Cain in envy slew him. When Jesus stood before Pilate on trial for His life, envy was there. Pilate was smart enough to know that it was present. We read, "For he (Pilate) perceived that it was out of envy that the chief priests had delivered Him up" (Mark 15:10). If people had not been envious there would never have been a cross on Calvary. When the religious leaders of Israel saw the foundation of their power and influence being cut from beneath their feet by Jesus Whom the multitudes were now following, they were overcome with the urge to destroy Him out of envy.

What Is Envy?

The envious person's attitude toward others is: "I don't want you to have what you have. If I can't have it, why should you?" How much of that rat-race called "keeping up with the Joneses" is nothing but envy!

There is an ancient legend about an envious man. Looking at his neighbor's successes and achievements with envious eyes, he cried out one day, "If only I could be successful and rich! Then I would be happy!"

Suddenly an angel appeared and said, "I am here to grant your every wish — on one condition."

"Yes, yes," answered our friend eagerly, "what's this condition?"

"Just this," answered the angel. "Every time you get something, your neighbor across the street will get twice as much. If you get a million dollars, he will immediately get two million dollars."

A cloud came over the man's face. Already he had become envious of the two million dollars which the neighbor did not have yet. After some deep thought, he told the angel sadly, "I cannot take your offer. It would not be worth it. Why should my neighbor get double of everything I want to have? That would

53

spoil everything.'' Sorrowfully, the angel left him stewing in his own juice.

The legend is not far fetched. We all have the urge to outdo the next person. There is nothing wrong with this *except* when it is born of envy.

Self-Destructive

There is an ancient Greek story about a man who killed himself through envy. His fellow citizens had created a statue to one of their number who was a celebrated champion in the Olympic games. But this man, a rival of the honored athlete, was so envious that he vowed he would destroy the statue. Every night he went out into the darkness and chiseled at its base in an effort to undermine its foundation and make it fall. At last he succeeded. It did fall — but it fell on him. He died, a victim of his own envy.

There is a story about a painting that shows how deadly envy is: On the wall of a chapel in Padua, an old city in northeastern Italy, is a painting by the Renaissance artist Giotto. On it he depicted Envy with long ears that could hear every bit of news of another's success. He also gave to Envy the tongue of a serpent to poison the reputation of the one being envied. But if you could look at the painting carefully, you would notice that the tongue coils back and stings the eyes of the figure itself. Not only did Giotto picture Envy as being blind but also as destroying itself with its own venomous evil. It always brings harm to the embittered person in whose heart it resides.

Envy was one of the sins that was hurting the church at Corinth. The people had divided into factions because they were jealous of one another's gifts. Each believer was striving for preeminence. Paul therefore instructed them to follow the "more excellent way" of love (I Cor. 12:31), telling them that "love envieth not" (I Cor. 13:4).

Satan's Subtle Tool

Envy is one of Satan's most subtle tools. A legend tells of the devil crossing the Libyan Desert when he met a number of his demons tempting a holy hermit. They tried to involve the hermit in sins of the flesh, but without success. He resisted steadfastly. Finally, after watching their failure in disgust, the devil whispered to his demons, "What you do is too crude. Permit me one moment." Then the devil whispered to the holy man, "Your brother has just been elected Patriarch of Alexandria." Immediately the hermit was overcome by envy. "That," said the devil to his crew, "is the sort of thing which I recommend to you."

It seems that the devil has been recommending and we have been busy following, or rather, falling victims to envy ever since.

How much of advertising today appeals to envy as a motive to make us buy a certain product? We are made to feel that if we buy a product our best friends will burn with envy. How many purchases have we made in the last 30 days that were prompted more by *envy* than by genuine need?

In another area of the business world, a guide to emotional problems prepared by the Connecticut Mutual Life Insurance Company says of the envious office worker: "How can he do his job if he lets envy strangle him? Think of the nervous energy he wastes worrying about what someone else is getting paid. Envy never increased anyone's salary."

Difference: Envy vs. Jealousy

As often as we may confuse them, there is a difference between envy and jealousy. Suppose you walk into a room and see a man kissing a beautiful woman. You may well envy the man. But if the woman he is kissing is your wife, you feel jealous.

Jealousy is involved where there is love. In envy we simply want something which belongs to someone else. You may envy a man his fine house without being jealous of him. In jealousy a loved one must be involved. This is why the Bible often speaks of God being jealous of us when, we who are loved by Him, bestow our allegiance on false gods.

The Cure For Envy

Is there no cure for envy? Are we merely to remain its victims and let it destroy our lives as well as the lives of others?

No! There is a cure. It is to the cure that we shall now turn our attention.

1. The first part of the cure is *empathy,* which means that we must enter into the other person's life as completely as we can. When we hear a violinist playing beautifully, instead of wishing we could play like that, we let the music of the violinist become our music as well. Empathy is the ability to make everyone's experience one's own. That way, life becomes so rich and full that there is very little place left for envy.

Inferiority

2. Pliny said once, "Envy, wherever it resides, always implies conscious inferiority." We envy other persons because we feel we are inferior to them. The cure for such inferiority and the envy to which it gives birth, is to count our blessings each day, to realize that there is something—at least one thing—which we can do supremely well. Our Lord may not have given all of us the same number of talents, but he *did* give each of us at least one talent. Remember what the little squirrel said to the great mountain: *"I* cannot carry forests on my back, but *you* cannot crack a nut." There will be little danger of envy if we make it a practice to count our blessings daily.

Do You See the Inner Wounds?

3. A really important question to ask is: how well do you really know the person you envy? Do you know his secret cares and wounds, his inner struggles? Have you ever prayed for him in love? If you have, then maybe you will come to see something of what goes on *inside* him which may be altogether different from what you choose to see in him when you enviously look only at the *outside* of him.

A banker once passed a gardener. As each went on his way, the gardener wished that he could be a banker, rich and happy. He'd sit in comfort in a chair behind his office walls and great important, busy men would come to him on urgent calls. But the gardener didn't know the banker's thoughts. All the while the banker was envying the gardener his glowing tan, his bright, clear eyes, his graceful stride and vim, "Oh, what a job,'' sighed the banker, ''to work near trees and roses, and breathe fresh air that hasn't been in other people's noses!''

Next time you are tempted to envy someone, ask yourself: Do I really know what goes on *inside* that person's heart?

Members of Each Other

4.   A fourth cure for envy is to realize that God created us to be members of His Body. Just as the members of our physical body need each other (the eye cannot say to the foot, ''I do not need you''), so as members of Christ's body, we need each other; we depend on each other. One of Aesop's fables illustrates this truth. It seems that the members of the body had a meeting one day. They decided to strike because the stomach was getting all the food while they were doing all the work. They soon discovered that when there was no food in the stomach, none of them could function. The story concludes: ''Even the stomach in its dull, quiet way is doing necessary work for the body, and all members must work together, or the body will go to pieces.'' Instead of being envious of the other person, accept him as a member of Christ's Body, who performs an important God-given function for you as well as for the whole body. Contentment, not envy, is the lifestyle of God's children.

A Cry For Love

5.   Envy has been called ''a cry for love.'' If you carry a crucifix around your neck, look at it once in a while and say, ''Jesus loves me. And He did that for me!'' It will be a sure cure for envy.

Prayer

6.   As with any sin, envy cannot be overcome without God's help. We need to get down on our knees daily and pray for God's strength. There was a preacher in London whose church was not as full as two neighboring churches who had famous preachers. The preacher confessed that he was tempted to be envious at times, but he took it to the Lord in prayer. ''When I prayed for their success,'' he said, ''the result was that

57

God filled their churches so full that the overflow filled mine, and it has been full since." Prayer is a potent cure for envy.

Love Casts Out Envy

7.   St. Paul writes, "Love does not envy . . ." (I Corinthians 13:4). Love overcomes envy. When Jesus started preaching, the great crowds left John the Baptist and followed Jesus. But there was no envy. Quietly and joyfully, John said, "He must increase, but I must decrease." No envy! Why? Because John loved Jesus. He loved Him with a great and passionate love and with true love there can be no envy.

8.   Finally, if you must envy someone, don't envy a successful millionaire or a beautiful actress. The millionaire probably has ulcers and the actress very likely is visiting a psychiatrist. Rather envy the person who has discovered the peace which the world cannot give. Envy those who are able to surrender their lives completely to God's loving care. Envy the person who lives out his days confident of God's forgiveness in Christ Jesus. Envy the old person on whose face is the light of eternal life. Envy the person who can honestly say with St. Paul, "I have learned in whatever state I am to be content."

The person most to be pitied is the one who envies others. He is already living in hell. The person most to be envied is the one whose great joy is to serve others. This person is already experiencing the bliss of heaven.

Jesus, Who was crucified because of envy, died to free us from its deadly manacles and give us a new life free from envy. May we repent of the terrible sin of envy, which destroys our peace. May we prostrate ourselves before the Cross of Jesus and pray:

> "O Christ, You Who were crucified because of envy, forgive my envy and heal my jealous heart. Fill me with Your love which casts out envy and makes me willing to serve my neighbor in love. Amen."

A WINDOW
OVER THE KITCHEN SINK
Palm Sunday.
John 12:1-18.

A few years ago a bad fire destroyed the farm house of a widow in Vermont. In rebuilding she was asked if there were any changes she wanted in the new house. She replied that the house could be rebuilt exactly as it was — with just one difference. She wanted a window over the kitchen sink.

For years she had washed dishes against a blank wall! Now she wanted a window to enable her to look out at the beautiful Green Mountains of Vermont. When you stop to think of it, this is what our Christian faith does for us. It puts a window over the kitchen sink. It gives us vision while we work.

All of us need vision. "Where there is no vision, the people perish," we read in the Book of Proverbs. A task without vision is drudgery. Every life that amounts to anything begins with a vision.

A Vision In Your Soul

"Moral education," said Dr. Alfred Whitehead, "is impossible apart from the habitual vision of greatness." And that is what worship is: the exposure of the soul to the highest that we know. We tend inevitably to grow like that to which we give our attention, our admiration and devotion.

A wise Indian father wished to give his property to that one of his three sons who showed the greatest prowess and promise. As a test, he pointed to a mountain and asked each of them to climb it and bring a token to show how far each had climbed up the mountain.

The first son returned with a white wild flower in his hands. The father knew that it grew only above the timberline. The second son brought a red flint stone which revealed to the father that he had made it almost to the top.

59

The third son was gone for a long time, and returned empty-handed. "Father, where I went," he explained, "there was nothing to bring back, but I stood at the summit and looked out upon a valley where two great rivers join the ocean."

And the proud father said to him, "It has been the ambition of my life that one of my sons should see what you have seen. You have nothing in your hand, but you have a greater thing: a vision in your soul. This is the greatest of all."

Great Visions

Let us look breifly at persons in the Bible who had great vision in their souls.

When King Darius ordered everyone in Babylon to worship no other God but the gods of Babylon, Daniel knelt three times a day in the privacy of his room, opened his window toward Jerusalem and prayed to the one true God. Morning, afternoon, and evening his window was opened toward Jerusalem. It was this vision of God nourished by prayer that enabled Daniel to remain faithful to God in pagan Babylon.

Isaiah's Vision

The prophet Isaiah had a great vision of God while he was in the Temple praying. "I saw the Lord high and lifted up and His train filling the Temple." Heavenly beings sang, "Holy, Holy, Holy, Lord God of Hosts. All the earth is full of thy glory." Standing there in the presence of God, Isaiah was overcome by sorrow for his sins. "I am a man of unclean lips, and I live among a people of unclean lips." God sent an angel to purge his lips with a burning coal. Forgiven, God commissioned him to speak in His behalf to the nation. Isaiah responded, "Here am I, Lord, send me." The vision of God that came to him while he was in the temple praying was the turning point in Isaiah's life.

Did not Christ make Isaiah's vision a reality for us? When we go forward to receive His Precious Body and Blood in the liturgy, do not the elements touch our lips like burning coals? As we hear the choir singing the same song of Isaiah's seraphim, "Holy, Holy, Holy is the Lord of hosts, the whole earth is full of His glory," does not the same High and Holy

God, unapproachable in glory, bend down to touch us in forgiveness and love through His Presence in the consecrated bread
and wine? Is it not with this vision in mind that we ought to
approach Christ in the Eucharist?

Stephen's Vision

As he was being stoned to death for his faith in Christ,
Stephen, one of the youngest, boldest and earliest followers of
Jesus, saw a vision. He looked up and said, "Behold, I see the
heavens opened, and the Son of man standing on the right hand
of God." He saw Jesus, and as he was dying he said, "Lord
Jesus, receive my spirit." And then rising to an even greater
height, drawn by the greatness of the vision he saw, he prayed
for those who were gnashing their teeth at him and stoning him,
"Lord, lay not this sin to their charge."

St. Constantine saw a vision of a flaming cross in the
heavens with the words "By this sign conquer." It was that
vision that led him to victory.

Paul's Vision

On the road to Damascus, Saul of Tarsus had a vision of
Christ. He heard His voice, "Saul, Saul, why do you persecute
me?" In the strength of that vision of Christ, Saul the persecutor
became Paul the Apostle. He never forgot that vision. Ridiculed
for his faith in Christ, *driven* from town to town, *shipwrecked,
stoned* and left for dead, *imprisoned, flogged* until his back
was covered with raw flesh, he speaks of "joy unspeakable."
"Thanks be to God who giveth us the victory," he writes. "In
all things we are more than conquerors." "God Who commanded the light to shine out of darkness has shined in our
hearts." "Thanks be to God for His unspeakable gift." The
secret of all this power, joy and love in Paul's life was the
heavenly vision. "I was not disobedient to the heavenly vision," he declared.

Jesus' Vision

Jesus Himself had a vision at the beginning of His public
ministry. As He came up out of the waters of Jordan at His

baptism, the heavens were opened and the Holy Spirit came upon Him in the form of a dove, filling Him with power. The voice of God the Father was heard saying, "This is my beloved Son in Whom I am well pleased." It was this vision that was to sustain Jesus through all His sufferings.

When Jesus was tempted, there was a vision of the Devil tempting Him; but this was not the whole vision. The other part was that of an angel whom God sent to minister to Him, to strengthen Him. It was the angel that brought Him God's support. In every temptation there is the Devil but there is also the vision of God's angel sent to provide a way out of the temptation. This is the vision that saves us!

Jacob's Vision

Jacob had a vision. He "dreamed that there was a ladder set up on the earth, and the top of it reached to heaven; and behold, the Lord stood above it and said, 'I am the Lord, the God of Abraham your father and the God of Isaac. . . . Behold, I am with you and will help you wherever you go, and will bring you back to this land; for I will not leave you . . .'" (Gen. 28:10 - 15). It was that vision that became the turning point in Jacob's life.

Jacob's vision became reality in Christ in Whom God Himself came down the ladder of heaven to be with us forever. God is no longer speaking to us from the top of the ladder as in Jacob's time. He is here with us at the bottom of the ladder, clothed in our own humanity. In Christ we have the vision of God with us in all the experiences of life — guiding, strengthening, forgiving.

Evagrius Ponticus, one of the desert fathers, called the life of prayer *theoria* (meaning vision) *physike* (of the nature of things), i.e., the vision of how things really hang together. The vision of how the entire universe hangs together in Christ (Col. 1:17). Jesus is God's pattern for life — for you and me. Let us not be disobedient to the heavenly vision.

"But I Have No Visions . . ."

Daniel, Isaiah, Stephen, Jacob, Paul, Jesus — all have shown that every life that amounts to anything begins with a

God-inspired vision. Already I can hear some saying, "But I have no visions; my life goes on rather monotonously and without much interest; I am past middle age, my mountain peaks are behind me; and I go about my job and try to do it as well as I can, but there is no excitement in me. I don't look for any new vision." Or you may be young, but your attitude is much the same: "I have never had any great visions; there is nothing that I particularly want to do in life; nothing has ever stirred those depths in me that you talk about in the lives of other people."

To these people let me say that God has given each one of us a vision in the light of His Gospel that stretches beyond this world. He has given us the vision to see what needs to be done in this world to bring love and grace into the drab lives of people.

"The sufferings of this present time are not worthy to be compared with the glory that is to be revealed to us," writes St. Paul. In Christ life has meaning. In Christ we have vision; we see the road ahead for what it is: the road to God, curving through tough country, it is true, but leading to a life which makes the whole journey worthwhile. This is the vision people need. Without it, they perish. This is the vision we need. Without it, life withers on the vine. This is the life-giving vision of Christ.

The Vision of Holy Week

Every year, for example, the Church comes with the beautiful worship services of Holy Week to offer us a vision of the length and breadth, the height and depth of the love of God Who spared not His own Son but gave Him up for our salvation. What sinner is there who does not need this vision of the God-man on the cross saying to each one of us, "Father, forgive them. . . . Today, you will be with me in Paradise." Do not say you have no vision. Every year God comes during Holy Week to give you a vision of His suffering love.

The Vision of Easter

As He comes during Holy Week with the vision of His love, so He comes to us at Easter with the vision of victory —

His and our victory over death. "I am the resurrection and the life, he who believes in me though he were dead yet shall he live." The news is so good that we cannot merely tell it; we sing it out: "Christ is risen from the dead, by His death He has trampled on death, and to those in the tombs He has bestowed life everlasting." Who is it who will not die? Who is it who does not right now have some loved one lying in a grave? Do not say you have no vision. Every year God comes at Easter to give us a vision of victory over our greatest enemy, a vision that dispels fear, a vision that lifts us to seek the things that are above.

The Vision of The Ascension

When forty days after Easter we see Jesus ascending into heaven, what is this but a vision of our own coming ascension to God? When we read God's Word in the Holy Bible, what is this but a vision of God speaking to us through His Word? When we open the windows of our soul to God every day through prayer as Daniel did, or worship God in the temple as Isaiah did, what is this but a vision of God? Without this vision we perish.

> *"Every morning lean thine arms awhile*
> *Upon the window sill of heaven*
> *And gaze upon thy Lord;*
> *Then with this vision in thy heart*
> *Turn strong to meet the day."*
>
> *(Author unknown)*

Our problem today is that we spend so much time watching TV and soap operas and X-rated movies that we have terrible visions, pornographic visions, lustful visions, visions that consist of the sewer backing up on us, visions that cheapen and degrade life. We need to keep our copy of the Bible on top of the TV set. When there's nothing good on TV, it's time to reach for the Bible and open it to let God fill our minds and hearts with noble visions that uplift and inspire. Many of us spend so little time with Jesus in church and in prayer and so much time watching sordid movies that our minds and hearts are literally polluted with constantly recurring visions of evil that haunt us. Jesus can liberate us from these terrible visions.

64

But we need to look prayerfully into the face of Jesus. He is our vision of God; our vision of what we should be; our vision of what by His grace we can be. "And we all, with unveiled face, beholding the glory of the Lord, are being changed into His likeness from one degree of glory to another . . ." writes St. Paul.

Vision and Task

The Christian life is made up both of visions and of tasks. As Phillips Brooks said, "It is a terrible thing to have no vision, but it is also a terrible thing to have seen the vision, and to be so wrapped up with its contemplation as not to hear the knock of needy hands upon our doors." The vision of God leads the Christian to tasks of love, i.e., the washing of feet, the feeding of the hungry, visiting the sick, clothing the naked. The vision of God in Christ and the task of love go hand in hand.

We assemble in Church on Sunday as God's people to have our vision sharpened. Here things should come into focus: what is the world like and what would God have us do. Vision and task go hand in hand, for faith without works is dead.

Vision From Worship

On a pew in a church in Brunswick, Maine, there is a brass plate with the inscription: "It was while seated in this pew, listening to her husband preach, that Harriet Beecher Stowe had the vision which led to the writing of 'Uncle Tom's Cabin.'" If the truth were known, might we not say, "It was while sitting in this pew that the heavens opened and someone like you and me had a vision of God which led to momentous changes in his life and the lives of those about him?

Grindstone Vision

We are told in an amusing poem that if we keep our nose to the grindstone long enough, "in time you'll say there is no such thing as brooks that bubble and birds that sing. These three will all your world compose, just you, your grindstone and your old nose." This is the kind of vision that comes from too much grindstone.

Vision More Than Science

Norman Cousins said once, "What holds men back today is not the pressure of realities, but the absence of dreams. If the dreams are good enough, no realities can stand against them. It was man's imagination . . . far more than his science that sent him to the moon." Vision!

A girl visiting her psychiatrist said, "Doctor, can't you give me something to look forward to?" A vision, a hope for the long future — this is what we must have — or we perish.

In one of the many art galleries of Europe, there is an old Greek statue of Apollo, a beautiful figure of physical perfection. Someone visiting the gallery said he didn't know which was more impressive to him, to look at the statue or to stand and watch the people as they looked at the statue. Invariably, he said, everyone who stood before it, even for an instant, began to straighten up, put back his shoulders, and stand tall — the lifting power of a vision of great beauty.

Jesus for Whom the heavens opened when He came up out of the waters, has never ceased to open heaven for us. He is our vision — a vision that makes us straighten up, push back our shoulders, and stand tall as God's children. Gaze upon Him faithfully each day. Open your soul to the vision He offers through prayer, the Bible, the Church. Then with the vision in your heart, turn strong to meet your day.

PRAYER

Lord, grant us vision,
- *the vision of Your love;*
- *the vision of Your victory over sin and death;*
- *the vision that we are Yours and that nothing can ever separate us from Your love;*
- *the vision of the greatness to which You call us as Your children;*
- *the vision that lifts us to seek things that are above.*
Amen.

YOUR BEST FRIEND
DIED TONIGHT
Good Friday.

If I were to summarize in a few words what happened on Good Friday, I would go where there are broken people, wounded people, poor people, oppressed people, lost people, forgotten people, sinful people, and I would say to them: "Your best Friend died tonight."

Who was ever a greater Friend than Jesus?

The greatest work that Jesus did was not at the marriage feast in Cana where He turned the water into wine.

The greatest work that Jesus did was not when He calmed the storm on the Sea of Galilee or came walking to Peter on the waves.

The greatest work that Jesus did was not when He made the blind to see, the deaf to hear, the dumb to speak.

The greatest work that Jesus did was not when He raised Lazarus who had been dead four days.

The greatest work that Jesus did was not when He taught as One having authority, or scathingly denounced the Pharisees for their hypocrisy.

The greatest work that Jesus did was not the great ethical program He brought to us.

The greatest work that Jesus did was not when He spoke in such a manner that those who heard Him said, "No man ever spoke as this man."

What then was His greatest work?

His greatest work was achieved in those dark hours on the cross at Calvary. Christ's greatest work was His dying for us.

"Greater love has no man than this, that a man lay down his life for his friends" (John 15:13).

Our best Friend laid down His life for His friends: you and me.

Who is this Friend?

Martyrdom or Sacrifice?

If He was man, His death was murder; if He was God, it was an offering.

If He was man, His death was martyrdom; if He was God, it was sacrifice.

If He was man, they took His life from Him; if He was God, He laid it down of Himself.

If He was man, we are called to admiration; if He was God, we are called to adoration.

If He was man, we must stand up and take our hats off; if He was God, we must fall down before Him and give Him our hearts.

"I lay down my life. . . . No one takes it from me, but I lay it down of my own accord. I have power to lay it down, and I have power to take it up again; this charge I have received from my Father," He said (John 10:17 - 18).

Who was this Friend? He was God! And He willingly laid down His life for us.

The Day of God's Grace

We call what God did for us in Christ on Good Friday "the grace of God." Grace means something completely and forever undeserved. It is love allowing itself to be punished when it is someone else who deserves to be punished. It is love accepting the death penalty of sin on behalf of the one who is really guilty. Grace is the Creator allowing Himself to be jeered, ridiculed, spat upon, judged at a mock trial, jabbed in the side with a spear, and sentenced to death for us. Grace is love favoring us when we are not favorable, accepting us when we are not acceptable, loving us when we are not lovable, redeeming us when we are not redeemable. In short, grace is Good Friday. It is our best Friend, Jesus, the Son of God, the Sinless One, dying on the cross for us, the sinful ones, that we may have life.

Not God's Anger But His Love

In history there have been those who have felt that Good Friday began with the anger of God. God was angry with sin

68

and His anger needed to be appeased. This is not what we find in God's word. "God so loved the world that He gave His only Son," we read. "God commends His love toward us in that while we were yet sinners, Christ died for us." Good Friday does not begin with God's anger but with His love.

God Shouts To Us From the Cross

C. S. Lewis said once, "God whispers to us in our pleasures, speaks in our conscience, but shouts in our pain. Pain is God's megaphone." On the cross God is in pain. It was a very unusual kind of pain which He knew He would have, which He foretold on many occasions. It was the pain that came from bearing on His shoulders the burden of all our sins. That is why He came to this earth. His very name, Jesus, means *Savior*: He saves us from our sins. He took on Himself the sin of each and every one of us.

If pain is God's megaphone and if God is in pain on the cross, He is indeed shouting to us through His pain. These are His words:

What More Can He Do?

"What more can I do for you? I placed you in paradise and you rebelled. I led you to the promised land and you turned against me. I sent the prophets to speak to you and you murdered them. Finally I came myself to speak to you in Person, to confront you personally with my love, and you crucified me. I rose from the grave to show you that I am indeed Lord of life and death. I established the Church, my mystical Body, through which I continue to be present to you today. I speak to you through the Bible. I have made myself present to you in the sacraments. I come to abide in you as often as you receive Me in Holy Communion. I have given you the privilege of prayer. I am present with you each Sunday in the liturgy, and every day in your prayers. What more can I do for you? For you I came down from heaven. For you I was mocked. For you I was scourged. For you I was spat upon. For you I am on the cross. To you I shout every Good Friday through my pain. Does God's love mean nothing to you? Is God's suffering in vain? Will you just stand there and admire or will you fall to your knees and

69

adore? Will you just tip your hat to your suffering Savior, or will you fall down and give Him your heart?

Your best Friend died tonight. It was not murder; it was an offering. It was not martyrdom; it was sacrifice. They did not take His life away from Him; He laid it down of Himself for your sins and mine, that we who believe in Him may not perish but have life.

When we look at the Cross on Good Friday, we know that God has gone as far as He can go in His love for us. Can He go any farther? Can He die again? How far will we go to meet that love?

PRAYER

Every member of Thy Body endured dishonor
for us:
    Thy Head, the thorns;
    Thy Face, the spittings;
    Thy Cheeks, the smittings;
    Thy Mouth, the taste of vinegar;
    Thine Ears, the impious blasphemies;
    Thy Back, the lash;
    Thy Hand, the reed;
    Thy Whole Body, extension upon the Cross;
    Thy Joints, the nails;
    And Thy Side, the spear;
    O Thou Who didst suffer for us, and set us
        free from suffering,
    Who by Thy compassion didst stoop down
        to raise us up,
    Almighty Savior, have mercy on us.   Amen.

CHRIST IS RISEN
Easter.

Christ is risen! The glorious message of life eternal! The message of victory and triumph! Christ is risen in power and majesty! And He proclaims the mighty truth: "All authority in heaven and on earth has been given to me."

Christ is risen! Gone the long, dark night! Gone the night's disappointments! Gone the night's fears! "Sorrow may endure for a night but joy cometh in the morning."

Christ is risen, replacing grief and sadness with the joyous truth that we are never alone, that even in sin, even in death, the Risen Christ is with us: "Lo, I am with you always even unto the end of the world."

Christ is risen! And because of it we have life not only beyond the grave but also before the grave. Fullness of life here and now! "As in Adam we all sin, so in Christ we are all made alive."

Christ is risen! And because He is risen, let no one ever tell you that you are terminal. You are not terminal but transitional. Those who believe in Jesus will one day pass not from life to death but from death to life. For the death of Jesus is the death of death.

Christ is risen! And because of it, the Gospel is true. As St. Paul writes, "If Christ has not been raised, your faith is empty and you are still in your sins. Then those who have fallen asleep in Christ have perished. If for this life only we have hoped in Christ, we are of all men most to be pitied. But in fact Christ has been raised from the dead, the first fruits of those who have fallen asleep. For as by a man came death, by a man has come also the resurrection of the dead" (I Cor. 15:17-21).

Christ is risen! And because of it we rise:

"Out of the tomb of doubt
        Into the light of faith;
    Out of the tomb of hate
        Into the light of love;

71

Out of the tomb of death
Into the light of life;
Out of the tomb of despair
Into the light of joy! (M. H. Hoyer).

Christ is risen! And because of it we sing on Easter morning toward the end of Matins: "It is the day of the Resurrection, let us be illumined by the Feast; let us embrace one another in love; let us call even those who hate us, our brothers. Let us forgive everything for the sake of the Resurrection, and so let us sing, 'Christ is risen from the dead, He has trampled down death by death and has given life to those who lay in the tombs.'"

Christ is risen! And because of it we know that we cannot ever destroy God's love. Even the ultimate rejection of God's love, the Cross, was God's very means of saying to us, "I love you and I will come to you with life."

Christ is risen! And because of it, says John Chrysostom: "The angels rejoice! Life reigns in freedom! And there is none left dead in the tomb!"

"The Lord is risen" smiled the sun. "The Lord is risen," sang the lark. And the church bells in their joyous pealing answered from tower to tower, "He is risen indeed" (Francis Kilvert).

Christ is risen! And because of it: "The light shines in the darkness and the darkness has not overcome it" (John 1:5). For this is not the light of some flickering candle. It is the light of Him Who said, "I am the light of the world: he who follows me will not walk in darkness but will have the light of life" (John 8:12).

Christ is risen! And because of it Paul says, "He has delivered us from the dominion of darkness and transferred us to the kingdom of His beloved Son, in Whom we have redemption, the forgiveness of sins" (Col. 1:13-14).

Christ is risen! And because of it we sing:

"Now are all things filled with light,
Heaven and earth and the places under the earth.
All creation does celebrate the Resurrection of Christ.
On Whom it is founded.

72

O Christ, the Passover great and most holy!
O Wisdom, Word and Power of God!
Grant that we may more perfectly partake of Thee
In the day of Thy Kingdom which knoweth no night.''

—From the Orthodox Easter Matins

SEEING IS BELIEVING
- - IS IT?

Sunday of St. Thomas.
John 20:19-31.

On the Sunday after Easter, noticing that the congregation was quite a bit smaller than the previous week, a pastor said, "Well, I see the Easter lilies are gone, but the perennials are still here."

In "Jesus Christ Superstar" the ruler tells Jesus, "Prove to me that you're divine, change my water into wine." Later he says, "Prove to me that you're no fool, walk across my swimming pool." There are those who are still asking Jesus to do the same thing for them. They are looking for another Houdini, not for a suffering Savior. They want some special miracle and sign, made and autographed in heaven and performed especially for them, before they will believe. They want God to jump when they say jump. And if He doesn't do exactly what they say, they won't believe. What they really want is to pin God down and make Him a puppet in their own hands.

Thomas wanted such a sign in today's Gospel lesson: "Unless I see in his hands the print of the nails, and place my finger in the mark of the nails, and place my hand in his side, I will not believe." He wanted to tie God down to seeing. Seeing is believing. "Unless I see and touch I will not believe," he said.

No Room For Faith?

People keep saying that there is no room in today's world for faith. Faith is a thing of the past. Today we have to live by what we see, hear and feel. Everything has to be proved in a test tube before it can be accepted. As if love, honesty, patriotism, honor, integrity, compassion can be placed in a test-tube and analyzed.

75

Seeing is believing — is it? Do you believe, for example, in photons? Maybe you don't know what they are. Physicists speak of a particle called a photon that doesn't exist unless it's traveling 186,000 miles per second (the speed of light), and is unobservable, one cannot see it, even though it does exist. In other words, science asks us to believe in the existence of photons even though we cannot see them, hear them, feel them, or even understand what they are.

Seeing is believing - - is it?

Major Trifoloff's Nemesis

One day Major Alexi Trifoloff of the Bulgarian Army marched his soldiers to the summit of a hill where he decided to take advantage of the view of Sofia to deliver a communist lecture.

"Comrade soldiers," he said, "do you see Sofia?"

"We see it."

"Do you see the Cathedral of Alexander Nevski?"

"We do."

"Do you see the mausoleum of the leader and teacher of the Bulgarian people?"

"We do."

"And do you see God, comrade soldiers?"

"We do not see Him, comrade major."

"Well then, this means, comrades, that there is no God. What cannot be seen does not exist. Sofia, the church of Alexander Nevski, the mausoleum; they are all here. You have not seen God; therefore He is not there. He does not exist. Understand?"

"We understand, comrade major."

Private Stoil Bojinoff, a peasant from a small country village, requested permission from the major to say something. Comrade major granted him permission. Stoil Bojinoff stood at attention in front of the soldiers.

"Comrade soldiers, do you see our major, comrade Alexi Trifoloff?"

"We see him."

"Do you see his boots, his sword, his strap?"

"We do."

76

"Do you see his head?"

"We do."

"Do you see his mind?"

"No, we do not see it."

"So it is comrade soldiers, as comrade major has told us: What one can see exists; what one cannot see does not exist. Understand?"

"We understand, comrade."

Seeing is believing - - is it?

Challenging God For Signs

One day a man who doubted whether God really existed looked up to the sky and said, "God, if You are really there, then make something special happen so that I can be sure." Then the man sat down to wait.

While he sat there the sun began to rise over a distant hill. And it colored everything in a scarlet hue. Then a tiny bird came, perched itself on a nearby tree and began to sing a beautiful song. Far down in the valley a farmer was harvesting a beautiful crop of wheat and on the road close by children were singing and playing as they walked to school.

The day passed on and the brilliant sun faded to the west and the stars came out. But still the man waited and nothing special seemed to happen. "There is no God," he said.

Seeing is believing - - is it?

Blind

"Show me your God!" the doubter cries.
I point him to the smiling skies;
I show him all the woodland greens;
I show him peaceful sylvan scenes;
I show him winter snows and frost;
I show him waters tempest-tossed;
I show him hills rock-ribbed and strong;
I bid him hear the thrush's song;
I show him flowers in the close—
The lily, violet and rose;
I show him rivers, babbling streams;
I show him youthful hopes and dreams;

77

I show him maids with eager hearts;
I show him toilers in the marts;
I show him stars, the moon, the sun;
I show him deeds of kindness done;
I show him joy; I show him care,
And still he holds his doubting air,
And faithless goes his way, for he
Is blind of soul, and cannot see!

John Kendrick Bangs

Seeing is believing - - is it?

A Sign From God

It is said that while the Germans were desecrating a church somewhere in Poland during World War II, a German sergeant stood up before the altar and shouted haughtily that if there was a God, He would want to prove His existence at once by striking down this terrible sergeant. Much to the sergeant's consternation God did not strike him down. For, you see, God had not acted like a Nazi. God was not in fact a Nazi and His justice is poles apart from the bloodthirsty revenge of the Nazis.

As for God's proving His existence with a sign, Jesus already told us that He would not give us a sign other than the greatest sign He ever gave us, i.e., that of His Resurrection: "An evil and adulterous generation seeks for a sign; but no sign will be given to it except the sign of the prophet Jonah. For as Jonah was three days and three nights in the belly of the whale, so will the Son of man be three days and three nights in the heart of the earth" (Matt. 12:38 - 39). No sign can ever be greater than this. If they will not believe the resurrection, they will not believe any other sign.

We Cannot See But We Are Seen

Yet people today are still asking the question Thomas asked:

"I can't see God. I can't hear God. I can't even reach out and touch to make sure God is there! How then can I trust God?"

78

A good question. And one that many people struggle with. How can I put faith in an unseen God? Listen to this true story about a family whose home caught fire in the middle of the night. The parents woke their children and quickly led them out. The five-year-old, however, slipped away and ran back upstairs. It wasn't until they were outside that they saw him in a second story window surrounded by smoke. The boy's father yelled, "Jump and I'll catch you!"

"But Daddy," the child protested, "I can't see you."

The father cried, "But I can see you and that's all that matters. Jump!"

Now it is true that we can't see God. When we are in pain, we can't see God. When desperately in need, we can't see God. When threatened by problems, broken relationships and disillusionment, we can't see God. But the important thing is that God can see us! And that's all that matters.

The faith by which and in which we live and which enables us to conduct our living and dying with dignity is not that we can see, but that we are seen; not that we can know without doubt, but that we are known through and through by the God Who is Lord of us in both our living and dying. For nothing can separate us from His love.

We Cannot Touch But We Are Touched

St. John Chrysostom said once, "Thomas doubted that we might have faith." The Apostle John defines faith as believing "that Jesus is the Son of God and that believing you might have life in His name." That kind of faith often comes through the crucible of honest doubt.

"Unless I touch with my finger the print of the nails . . . I will not believe." That's what Thomas said before he saw Jesus. But he did not have to touch Jesus when He appeared. Instead he himself *was touched by the Risen Christ!* What Christ is looking for is faith. Throughout history people of faith have been touched by the risen and living Christ. Touched with forgiveness. Touched with power. Touched with love. Touched with hope. They did not need any more proof. You can see it in their lives, as you can see it in Thomas. Touched by Jesus he confessed: "My Lord and my God!" That changed everything in his life.

To Believe Is To See

"Did I not tell you," said Jesus to His disciples one day, "that if you *believed* you would *see* . . ." *"If you believed, you would see* greater miracles than the ones I have performed." Seeing is believing? Nothing of the kind! It is the *believing that is the only seeing!* said Jesus. It is the person who believes who truly sees. He sees God all around him. The whole universe becomes a sacrament, a burning bush. He sees purpose and meaning in life. He sees who he really is. He sees God in Christ, and believing in Him he has life in His name. St. Augustine wrote, "Faith is to believe what we do not see. And the reward of this faith is to see what we believe."

Believing is seeing! Saul was blind until he met Christ on the road to Damascus. He believed and his eyes were opened. For the first time in his life he saw the one true God and the plan God had for his life. Faith itself is sight. To believe is to see.

"Have you believed because you have seen me?" Jesus asked Thomas. "Blessed are those who have not seen and yet believe."

Faith — not seeing — is the real miracle. It is when we believe that we truly see. "All I have seen teaches me to trust the Creator for what I have not seen," said Emerson.

PRAYER

I pray for the gift of faith, dear Lord, that I may truly see. Amen.

80

JOSEPH OF ARIMATHEA
. . . TOOK COURAGE
AND WENT TO PILATE
Sunday of the Myrrh-Bearers.
Mark 15:43 - 16:8.

Jesus is dead. His limp body hangs on the cross between the bodies of the two dead thieves. Who will claim the body of the Person against Whom a whole nation had vented its rage? Who will have courage enough to appear before Pilate and ask for the body of an executed "criminal"? His disciples? Where were they to be found? They were in hiding for fear of their lives. But there was another disciple. He was a disciple of Jesus in secret, "a respected member of the council, who was also himself looking for the kingdom of God." But now he declared himself openly for Jesus. "Joseph of Arimathea . . . *took courage* and went to Pilate, and asked for the body of Jesus." It took courage — unusual courage — for a person to do that.

Many Kinds of Courage

There are many kinds of courage. There is the courage we see on the battlefield. There is the courage we see in perilous rescues. There is the courage shown by astronauts. There is the courage of the early Christians who, rather than deny Christ, suffered to have their bodies dipped in tar and used as flaming torches to provide light for the Roman festivals. There is the courage of the 40 holy martyrs who were left to freeze to death naked on a frozen lake rather than surrender their faith. There is the courage of Christians today in Communist-held countries where those who refuse to deny Christ are subjected to indescribable torture in concentration camps. This, we say, is courage! It is something defiant. It is walking through flames. It is standing up to physical dangers.

But there is another kind of courage — a courage which is quiet but firm, a courage which in time of crisis reveals itself in the ability to say yes or no — and to say it firmly; a courage which belongs to the art of living. Following the recent suicide of a Hollywood actress, a woman in Rome remarked, "She must have had wonderful courage to die like that," to which someone replied, "Perhaps she did not have the courage to live." There are times when it takes courage to live. When the storms beat about us and bright days seem more like dark nights, it takes courage to live.

The Courage of Going On

It takes courage such as is never seen on the battlefield to live doing what we have to do, not what we like to do, but what love and duty and compassion demand of us. To face the new day with the knowledge that it will be another day just like yesterday with the same burdens, the same problems, the same heartaches. That takes courage!

When asked what kind of heroism she practiced, one elderly scrubwoman replied, "I practice the heroism of going on."

Courage to Repent

It takes courage to strip ourselves of the masks we wear, to see ourselves as we really are and to do something about it. When the prodigal son said to his father, "I have sinned against heaven and before you. I am no longer worthy to be called your son," at that moment he walked in the dust over his pride. That took some courage. But when he said to himself while still in that far country, "I will arise and go to my father," he showed the greater courage. It takes courage to admit one's sin. But to actively rise, to forsake our sin and return to the Father, that always takes the greater courage.

It takes courage to be a Christian in today's world. The road of the Christian is hard. The way of the Christian is not popular. It takes courage to follow Jesus in our everyday life. It takes courage to maintain a Christian home. It takes courage to live by Christian standards. There can be no true Christian today without courage. What is the source of this courage? How do we get it? Where do we find it?

The Source of Courage

When Daniel was forbidden by decree of Nebuchadnezzar to pray to his God, he not only continued to kneel and pray three times a day as was his custom; but he continued to perform this ritual before his open window, as he did before, where all might see, fully aware that he would be cast into the den of lions as punishment. What was the source of Daniel's courage? It was prayer! Three times a day he opened his window toward Jerusalem and prayed to the one true God. He stood by the Lord and the Lord stood by him even when he was cast into the lion's den.

In writing of the early Christian martyrs an anonymous author wrote:

"Who can choose but admire their nobility and endurance and love for the Master. I speak of the men who were so tortured with whipping that their bodies were laid open to their veins and arteries, yet they endured it, so that all who saw them pitied and lamented their fate. Not one of them sighed or groaned, *for the Lord stood by them and consoled them."*

Here, then, was the secret of their remarkable courage: *"the Lord stood by them . . ."*

Spend Time With Jesus

The New Testament says that when they saw the boldness of Peter and John, they took note of them that they had been with Jesus. There is something about spending time in the presence of Jesus that puts iron into our blood. It strengthens us not to fear the faces of men. For courage is more than bravado. It comes from the depths of our soul when we know deep down that God is with us.

This is why courage comes from hanging on to the promises of God. The Bible is the wisest book ever written. It has a great deal to say about courage. Take this single promise, for example, from Joshua 1:9, "Be strong and of good courage; be not afraid, neither be dismayed; for the Lord your God is with you wherever you go." No matter how many difficult and dark moments you face in life, if you hang on to that promise that God is with you, and feed your soul on it, you will overcome.

Relinquishment

Listen for a moment to this personal testimony from the life of Dr. Martin Luther King on how he found courage in a moment of weakness:

>"*I bowed over the kitchen table and prayed aloud. . . . I am here taking a stand for what I believe is right. But now I am afraid. . . . I am at the end of my powers. I have nothing left. I've come to the point where I can't face it alone. At that moment I experienced the presence of the Divine as I had never experienced Him before. It seemed as though I could hear the quiet assurance of an inner voice saying: Stand up for righteousness, stand up for truth, and God will be at your side forever. Almost at once my fears began to go. My uncertainty disappeared. I was ready to face anything.*"

A tremendous surge of courage came to Dr. King after he relinquished it all to the Lord in prayer.

Filled With the Holy Spirit

We must think courage and pray courage. And above all, never take counsel of our fears. Always take counsel of courage which grows in the soul as we anchor our lives on the solid rock which is Jesus. We love Him enough to know that He will never abandon us.

We read in Acts 4:13, "Now when they saw the boldness of Peter . . . they marvelled." When we look back to verse eight we find the secret of Peter's boldness: "Then Peter was filled with the Holy Spirit!" That was the source of Peter's boldness. It is Peter filled with the Holy Spirit! A person who is filled with the Holy Spirit can be none other than bold.

They Had Been With Jesus

Another source of the boldness of Peter is brought out in Acts 4:13, "They recognized that they (Peter and John) *had been with Jesus*." The presence of Jesus begets and nourishes boldness in His disciples.

A story is told of a missionary to the Indians who was a giant of a man — six feet six inches tall. Captured by a tribe that rejected his ministry, he suffered untold tortures. Finally he was scalded with boiling water in a mockery of baptism. But so staunch was his faith that he did not flinch.

The Indians were overwhelmed by the strength and courage of this man. At the end they tore his heart out, eating his flesh and drinking his blood, thinking in that way they would be able to share his strength and spirit.

The Lord Jesus wants us to have His courage. That is why He invites us to eat His flesh and drink His blood, not in the crude way those Indians did, but in the wonderful way devised by the love of God. "He who eats my flesh and drinks my blood lives in Me and I in him." Christ living in us, as He did in the apostles, instills courage.

What Is Courage?

We all thrill to the magnificent reply made by the three hundred Spartans the night before Thermopylae when they were told by a spy that the arrows of the Persians would be so many they would darken the sun. "Splendid, " they exclaimed, "then we shall fight in the shade!" That is courage!

In the orient the plum tree is a symbol of courage. When asked why, a person received this answer: "Because it puts out its blossoms while the snow is still on the ground." That is courage!

Noticing a buttercup thrusting itself up through the blackness of a forest floor that had been destroyed by fire, a person said, "That is courage!"

"Courage is the finest of human qualities," said Winston Churchill, "because it guarantees all the others." Life shrinks or expands in proportion to one's courage.

Parrhesia

The word for boldness in the Greek language is *parrhesia*. It comes from two Greek words *pas,* meaning *all,* and *rheo* meaning *to flow* or *to utter.* So the word means that a person who has the boldness of Christ is not afraid to speak, but proclaims the gospel of Jesus boldly and freely. We have to be bold for Christ because upon our boldness depends the whole cause of the Kingdom of God. The salvation of the world demands our boldness. Fearful Christians will never bring in the Kingdom of God. Timid Christians cringing in the closet, fearful to speak the name of the Master will never overthrow the strongholds of evil.

Speaking at Harvard a few years ago when he gave the graduation address, Alexander Solzhenitsyn noted that a decline in courage is the most salient feature of what he called "the spiritual exhaustion of the West." He went on to say, "To defend yourself, one must be ready to die; there is little such readiness in a society raised in the cult of material well-being." He berated America's lack of moral courage.

Closet Christians

It seems today that everybody has left the closet. The fornicators have left the closet. Those who lived together in the past were living in sin; now they are called "swingers." They even put their names boldly on the mailbox for all to see: "John Jones and Mary Smith." The prostitutes have left the closet. They are now out in the streets demanding their rights. The same is true for the homosexuals. No longer in the closet, they are marching in the streets demanding "gay rights."

There is practically no one left in the closet any more *except . . . except* a large group still hiding in the shadowy darkness. Who are they? Christians! They are practically the only people left in the closet. They are afraid to let the world know that they are followers of Jesus. They hide their faith in the shadow of the closet. While the Christians are in the closet, the atheists and the secular humanists are out turning the world upside down. Joseph of Arimathea was a "closet" Christian, but he "took courage" to leave the closet and declare himself publicly for Jesus, asking Pilate for the body of Jesus. The Christian belongs in the closet only for prayer (Matt. 6:6). Then he must leave the closet to confess Christ and work for Him in the world.

Were the early apostles "closet" Christians when they defied kings, laughed at princes, and died for what they preached?

86

Was Paul a "closet" Christian when he stood in the arena in Ephesus where everybody was shouting "Great is Diana of the Ephesians" and proclaimed publicly "Great is Jesus of Nazareth"?

Was John the Baptist a "closet" Christian when he denounced the immorality and corruption of a royal court, even though he knew it must cost him his head?

Was Marshal Foch, Commander-in-chief of the Allied Forces in World War I, a "closet" Christian when he made the sign of the cross publicly and prayed before every meal?

Courage In Suffering

The presence of God in us banishes fear and produces courage even in severe suffering. Listen to this story by Archbishop Helder Camara:

"A very beautiful friend of mine had fallen ill. She asked me as her confessor to pay her a visit.

"She lay in bed, allowing only half of her face to be seen. With a smile she said: 'Summon up your courage and don't be frightened.' Then she showed me the other half of her face, terribly eaten by cancer.

"I stood there in shock. How could cancer have been so insolent as to mar such beauty? Still smiling, she asked me to celebrate holy Mass there in her bedroom, because she wanted to unite her poor little suffering to the infinite suffering of God's Son, Jesus our Brother.

"We can grow, mature, enrich ourselves through suffering. We can continue to hope in the midst of suffering!"

We can have courage in the midst of suffering if we invite Jesus to be with us. There is nothing like a relationship with Jesus Christ to give us courage. If He is your Friend, you can know that when you walk through the waters, they will not overflow; when you go through the fire, it will not consume you; and when the darkness begins to come, it will lead to a dawn more glorious than ever!

PRAYER

Without You, Heavenly father, we are weak, empty, fearful, powerless. With You, we can face life boldly and with courage. Thank You for the boldness You have given us to approach You in prayer, and to call You "Our Father," and to find in You a Father Who loves, cares, empowers and emboldens. Amen.

PEOPLE WHO NEED PEOPLE
Sunday of the Paralytic.
John 5:1-15.

A "Peanuts" cartoon showed Lucy playing the psychiatrist. Seated behind her little counter under the sign "Psychiatric Help, 5¢," she was dealing with Charlie Brown. Said he, "I don't know what to do . . . sometimes I get so lonely I can hardly stand it. . . . Other times, I actually long to be completely alone . . ." Lucy gave him some direct counseling: "Try to live in between . . . five cents, please."

Charlie Brown voices the plight of many people today. Loneliness causes much distress. "Sir, I have no man" — the words of the paralytic in today's Gospel lesson — are the words of much of suffering humanity. Great cities, as well as small urban centers, can be locations of deep loneliness. We may experience what one has called "proximity without community." In our rapidly increasing high-rise apartment complexes, a person can be carried out in his coffin and the notice of his death be the first hint his neighbors may have had that he ever lived.

Walling Ourselves In

Of course, there are times when we ourselves bring on the loneliness. By our personal attitude of aloofness we make it almost impossible for people to get to us, and then we cry out against the unfriendly folk about us. We literally wall ourselves in and then criticize our neighbors because they do not climb over the walls to come and see us.

Only when loneliness leads us to tear down the walls and build good relationships to others is loneliness good. One of the functions of the Church is to be a loving, caring community that reaches out to the suffering and the lonely. Let me share with you the experience of a minister friend:

Loneliness Overcome

"My mother died when I was four years old. One of the persons who saved me from utter devastation in the aftermath of that experience was the old lady next door. I suppose she brought a hot dish, but she brought far more. She brought herself. I had no claim upon her whatsoever. We were not related. We were Wisconsin folk; she was from Norway, 'the old country.' My father was a school teacher; she had almost no education. But 'Grandma Lee' knew me — and my brothers and my dad — as people who needed people. And so her home was my home, her fresh-baked bread was my bread of life after school, her place was where I could go when I was sick or lonely or afraid and dad wasn't home from work yet — in short, her love was my sustaining strength. In part, it was through her that I became a *person*. In part, it was because of Grandma Lee that I knew what my Sunday School teacher was talking about when she gave me a gold star for memorizing, 'God is Love.'"

It was wonderful to have someone like Grandma Lee. It is even more wonderful to *be* someone like her. It is wonderful to be needed and to be able to serve others. Unfortunately in this day and age some people are too busy building walls around themselves. But when the chips are down, people still need people. Christ calls on us to build bridges to others — bridges that overcome loneliness and lead to fulfillment in life.

Too many loved and potentially lovable persons are like Willy Loman in Arthur Miller's play, "Death of a Salesman." In his sixties Willy loses his job, is overwhelmed by despair. He can't make it alone. One night when his son takes him out for the evening, Willy's wife speaks quietly to her son, "Be kind to your father, son. He is only a little boat looking for a harbor." Christ is searching for all little lost boats. He longs to lead them into the harbor of His forgiveness, of His acceptance, of His love. He has entrusted to us the task of inviting them to His harbor.

The cry of loneliness, "Sir, I have no man," is still heard in our world today. It is a painful cry — yet a cry that presents us with a Christian challenge.

Barbra Streisand, in *Funny Girl,* sang, "People who need people are the luckiest people in the world." Upon hearing these words, someone prayed, "Lord, I know how much I need people. Help me to find the people who need me. Amen."

MAKE IT PERSONAL
The Samaritan Woman.
John 4:5 - 42.

We live in a society in which we are identified by numbers. We are a social security number to the government. Another number identifies us at our place of employment. We are a number in college and a number in the armed forces. We are told that computer cards can translate all of our personality into numerical digits by which we can be sorted and identified. We are told that one day we may receive mail addressed to our social security number, followed by street number and finally a zip code.

One person examined his billfold and discovered that he carried credit cards and identification numbers totaling twenty-one different sets of numbers by which he is known. We can sympathize with the person who said, "I have finally learned how to get attention. When I receive a computer card, I fold, spindle and mutilate it. Then it stops the whole machine, and they learn my name and discover I am a person."

Paul Tournier said once, "The more we fill our universe with machines, the more important it is that we treat each other as persons."

A successful defense attorney was asked once how he managed to win so often in court. He replied, "Tell the jury about Tom Jones or Bill Green. I never refer to them as 'the defendant' or 'my client.' I've found that juries will hang defendants and clients but that they are not so anxious to hang Tom Jones or Bill Green." This successful attorney had discovered the importance of "making it personal."

The Greatness of God

Mrs. Humphrey Ward, the British novelist, once wrote to a member of Parliament telling him of the needs of a family among his constituents. She asked him to give the family his

91

attention. He replied that he was so busy with the human race that he had no time for the individual. That night Mrs. Ward wrote in her diary, "Our divine Lord, when last heard from, had not attained this sublime attitude." The greatness of our God is that even though He rules the universe, we are not numbers to Him. He has time for, and listens to, and cares for each one of His children individually and personally.

Not As Crowds But As Persons

The Lord Jesus demonstrated often that He thinks of us not as crowds and masses but as persons and individuals. He loves us as if there were only one of us in this universe. And as far as He is concerned there is only one of us because each one of us is unique. In this vast universe there is no one exactly like us. The very hairs of our head are numbered and known to God. He knows each one of us personally. He calls us by name. And He is concerned about each one of our needs. If Christ's ministry among us had any purpose, it was to demonstrate God's personal love for people. Jesus made God's love personal:

> to friendless Zacchaeus sitting alone up a tree;
> to the blind beggar lying by the roadside, crying for help;
> to the woman who touched the hem of His robe seeking healing;
> to the adulteress who was about to be stoned for her sin;
> to the father who came pleading in behalf of his sick daughter;
> to the thief who was crucified next to Him,
> and to the Samaritan woman whom He met by the well.

His hours were full, yet He was never too busy to spend time with individuals to show them that God cared personally for each one of them.

A Personal Encounter

Let's concentrate for a moment on the story of our Lord's encounter with the Samaritan woman. In those days a Rabbi was not allowed even to greet a woman in public—much less a Samaritan woman with whom the Jews were not on speaking terms. A Rabbi at the time of Jesus was not permitted to speak even to his wife or daughter or sister in public. There were even Pharisees who were called "the bruised and bleeding Pharisees" because whenever they saw a woman on the street they shut their eyes and so walked into walls and houses! For a Rabbi to be seen speaking to a woman in public was the end of his reputation—yet Jesus spoke to this woman. Not only was she a Samaritan and a woman; she was also a woman with a bad reputation. No decent man, let alone a Rabbi as Jesus was, would have been seen in the company of a Samaritan, especially a woman, especially a woman with a bad reputation. After listening as she poured out the sorry story of her life, Jesus offered her the water of life "of which if any man drink, he shall never thirst again." Here is a picture of God making His love for people personal. For, what can be more personal than the conversation Jesus had with the Samaritan woman at the well?

"Who Touched Me?"

When a woman touched Him in a crowd one day, Jesus asked, "Who touched me?" His disciples were often in crowds that meant little to them. They were amazed at His question and said, "In all this crowd You want to know who touched You?" But Jesus didn't want anyone to get lost in a crowd. He didn't want anyone to be treated impersonally.

How much we need to make the love of Christ personal to people today. It was said of a preacher that each person in his audience felt as though the message was intended for him and for him alone. Frank Laubach, the great Christian apostle of literacy, suggests that we throw one arm up vertically to receive Christ's love and throw the other arm out horizontally to aim this love that we receive from Christ to other people.

"Pick Up the Phone and Call Me"

Let us see how we can make the love of Christ personal to people.

Recently I read the story of a man who had to go through the Mayo Clinic in Rochester. It impressed me because it illustrates how personal we can make our concern for others. After being admitted to the Clinic, this man said, he was ushered into a doctor's small office. Each patient at Mayo is assigned to a doctor who becomes his "anchor man" regardless of how many other specialists he sees. The doctor came in, introduced himself, and said, "This is a big place. You feel lost here. But I want you to know that every facility of the Clinic is here for one purpose — to serve you." He took out a card, wrote down a number and said, "If you need me any hour of the day or night while you are here, pick up the phone in your room, call this number, and I'll be at your side within five minutes." The patient went on to say, "That did something for me. I felt that I was not part of an impersonal machine; I was the most important element here. I knew that someone cared. Already, I felt better."

As I read this story I thought, "Isn't that exactly the kind of love we Christians should have?" Our love for people should be personal — deeply personal — as personal as the love Jesus had for the Samaritan woman and has for every one of us; at least as personal as what that Mayo doctor gave his patient."

Other Examples of Personal Caring

A Muslim student on an American college campus said, "It was not until I understood that my roommate was really interested in me as a person that I began to see what his Christianity was all about." Christ's love is personal.

Augustine wrote about the person who was most instrumental in converting him to Christianity, Bishop Ambrose of Milan, "That man of God received me as a father and showed me kindness. I began to love him, at first not as a teacher of truth, but as a person, a person who was kind to me." Bishop Ambrose made the love of God personal to Augustine.

Dr. Karl Menninger, the great psychiatrist, tells of a woman patient whom he calls Mary Smith. She was in a mental hospital for years and was given up as hopeless. One day a new doctor was placed in charge of her ward. He made a systematic effort to become personally acquainted with each patient —

among them — Mary Smith. He paid attention to her. He noticed her as a troubled human being. He listened to her attentively. He went on walks with her. He showed a deep, personal concern for her. As a result, Mary Smith began to show improvement — marked improvement. Shortly thereafter she was released from the hospital to return to her family completely well. The greatest factor in her healing according to Dr. Menninger was the doctor's deep concern for her as a person.

A physician said of a large hospital in Germany, "I think I can say that my hospital is pervaded by a personal spirit, but I believe we owe this almost entirely to a single person — our Sister Superior, who is so profoundly human that everyone whose life she touches feels that he is considered a person." He went on to say that her secret was her personal communion with Jesus. This was the source of her very warm, personal love for people.

Personal Caring In the Home

A certain author tells how he goes about making his love for his wife personal. Once a week they go out to dinner alone so that they may have time to look deeply into each other's soul. And each day they spend at least fifteen minutes visiting in depth, listening to each other, sharing their mutual hopes, surfacing their hostilities, discussing their worries, praying together. If we make time for such undistracted personal encounters, we shall discover a wonderful way to keep love growing in marriage.

The same author goes on to say that each month he takes each child out to dinner alone. Often it's just for a hamburger. Father and son or daughter sit down alone and discuss whatever is on their minds. Mostly dad listens to junior's troubles. I cannot think of a better way to make parental love personal to children.[1]

Small Prayer Groups

In our parish we have small Bible study and prayer groups. The purpose of these groups is to make the love of Christ more

---

[1] "Promises to Peter" by Charlie Shedd. Word Books. Waco, Texas.

personal. When ten or twelve people meet together in a circle for prayer and Bible study, they begin to sense that they are members "one of another." In a group such as this, no one is a number, part of an impersonal mass of people. For each one, prayer is something which he does and the meaning of the Bible verses we read is something we all share. Each one speaks as he is led, sharing experiences that are meaningful to all of us. The love of Christ becomes personal in the sharing, caring and praying of such small groups.

How personal was the love of Jesus for the Samaritan woman and for all who came into contact with Him. May we throw up one arm each day in prayer to receive the love of Christ and then throw the other arm out horizontally to aim this love that we receive from Jesus to the people we meet every day, beginning with the members of our own family. It cannot but revolutionize our lives and the world.

PRAYER

As Your love for us is so deeply personal,
Help us, Lord, to treat each other not as numbers
    but as special persons,
Created in Your own image,
Deeply loved by You.
Destined to spend eternity with You. Amen.

THE REDEMPTIVE USE
OF SUFFERING

The Healing of the Man Born Blind.
John 9:1 - 38.

"Rabbi, who sinned, this man or his parents, that he was born blind?" Jesus answered, "It was not that this man sinned or his parents, but that the works of God might be made manifest in him."

Jesus shares with us in the Gospel lesson today two great facts. Fact number one: the cross is a fact of life. Suffering is part of life. It is unavoidable. It will come to us. No one can escape it. Sinner and saint — all suffer. God had only one Son and even He was not spared suffering.

But suffering is not the only fact. It does not stand alone. There is a second fact that is related to it, i.e., that suffering can be used redemptively. Good can come out of it. It can be positive. God can be glorified through suffering. The person in the Gospel lesson today was blind. That was the fact of human suffering. But that fact did not stand alone. There was another fact brought out by Jesus when He said that through this man's blindness "the works of God would be made manifest." Bringing His light to bear on this man born blind, He Who is the Light of the World, dispelled the darkness. And God was glorified through this great miracle.

The Important Question

The important question here is not: "How come this man is blind? Is it because of his sins or the sins of his parents?" The really important question is this: Now that his terrible situation is a fact, what do I do about it? How can I let God in on it, so that He may assume control? For in every situation, however dark, that is always possible. The works of God can be manifested right now in my life and in my suffering, if I relinquish my life to God. God is the One Who makes the difference. He is the One Who helps us use suffering in a positive and creative way. The suffering of Jesus on the Cross was positive, creative and redemptive because Jesus surrendered His suffering to the Father. Because of this we are assured that there are no irreparable disasters when faith takes charge. There are no situations where there does not exist the opportunity of glorifying God. For the true Christian, no experience in life is wasted. "All things (including suffering) work together for good to those who love God" (St. Paul).

The Transfiguration of Suffering

With God's help, we can truly turn our scars into stars. Jesus came not to justify suffering or to explain it but to transfigure it into a positive experience; to transform the greatest symbol of the world's evil — the cross — into a plus sign!

How can suffering be transfigured? What possible good can come from pain and suffering?

Let us see.

A great saint said once, "God instructs the heart, not by ideas, but by pain." Strength is born not in joy but in the deep silence of long-suffering hearts. No affliction would truly trouble a child of God, if he knew God's reason for sending it. And that reason is always one of love.

The Great Saints Speak

Listen to the Apostle James:

"Count it all joy, my brethren, when you meet various trials, for you know that the testing of your faith produces steadfastness. And let steadfastness have its full effect, that you may be perfect and complete, lacking in nothing" (James 1:2-4).

Listen to the Apostle Paul:

"More than that, we rejoice in our sufferings, knowing that suffering produces endurance, and endurance produces character, and character produces hope, and hope does not disappoint us, because God's love has been poured into our hearts through the Holy Spirit which has been given to us" (Romans 5:3-5).

Listen to the Psalmist:

"Before I was afflicted I went astray; but now I keep thy word. . . . It was good for me that I was afflicted, that I might learn thy statutes" *(Psalm 119:67, 71).*

"It was not that this man sinned, or his parents, but that the works of God might be made manifest in him."

He Makes Me To Lie Down

We read in the Shepherd Psalm that the Good Shepherd made his sheep to lie down in green pastures. Have you ever been flattened out by God on a bed of pain where He forces you to stop all your activities, to lie on your back helpless and weak so that you may look up to Him. The pastures on which He makes us lie are green. They are fertile and productive because through prayer and the Eucharist God is with us all the way. He sees to it that all things, even our lying down, work for good to those who love God and cooperate with Him. He transfigures suffering turning it into a redemptive experience for us where the works of God are made manifest and God's name is magnified.

As one terminally ill patient said to her uncle, "Oh, Uncle Harold, I wish you could know the sweet peace that I know now. But you can't because you are so full of health. You can't know until you get this sick, how good God can be."

Rising Above the Storms

E. S. Jones described an experience he had once in India:

' "Once I watched an eagle in the Himalayan mountains face a storm. It was a heavy storm brewing at the edge of the valley. I wondered what the eagle would do as the storm rushed through the narrow valley. Would it fly above the fury of the storm? Would it be dashed to pieces on the rocks below? No! It set its wings in such a way that the air currents sent him above the storm by their very fury. He didn't bear the storm; he used it to reach greater heights. We must learn that lesson of turning all resistance into opportunity, turning all resistance into release. Then you know how to live. It was the set of wings with the eagle that made the difference. This is a victorious way to live."[1]

This is exactly what God does when we let Him into our suffering. He helps us rise above it. He takes an experience that can make us bitter and uses it to make us better. He transforms and transfigures the cross into a plus sign. God's works are made manifest. His power is revealed and His name glorified.

We Choose the Color!

Dr. Harry Emerson Fosdick once had in his congregation a lovely lady who had spent most of her life on beds of pain. During a particularly trying time a sympathetic friend said to her, "Trouble does so color our life, doesn't it?" Quick as a flash, she replied: "Yes, trouble does color life, but I choose the color," and she had chosen "The red of courage and the gold of faith that are woven when ere a man looks in the face of trouble and does the best he can."

That is victory!

Michael J. Dowling, without arms and without legs, became the leading citizen of his community, living a happy, creative and useful life. One night his city paid him special tribute for his amazing achievements. He thanked them for their kindness and said: "I thank God I am not a cripple. I believe I have proved conclusively that to be a cripple is not a condition of body but a state of mind."

That is victory!

A man who had lost his eye and had to have a glass eye said to his doctor, "If you have to give me a glass eye, please put a twinkle in it."

That is victory!

A great Christian who had been years upon her bed with acute arthritis said of herself, "I'm in Nero's prison but I am not Nero's prisoner." Most of her great books came out of the

---

[1] "The Divine Yes," E. S. Jones. Abingdon Press, Nashville, TN. 1975. p. 101.

period when she was an invalid. She was not a prisoner of arthritis. She rose above it.

That is victory — Christ's victory over suffering.

A Hard Boiled Egg or A Soft Potato?

Speaking of the lessons she learned from a tragedy in life one mother said, "While my husband Frank and I were living in Pakistan many years ago, our six-month-old baby died. An old Punjabi who heard of our grief came to comfort us. 'A tragedy like this is similar to being plunged into boiling water,' he said. 'If you are an egg, your affliction will make you hard boiled and unresponsive. If you are a potato, you will emerge soft and pliable, resilient and adaptable.' It may sound funny to God," said his mother, "but there have been many times when I have prayed, 'O Lord, let me be not a hard-boiled egg but a potato.'"

The Great Difference

Thus, the blind man in today's Gospel lesson brings us face to face not only with the fact of suffering but also with the fact that Jesus can transform suffering into a positive and redemptive experience. God uses suffering and pain to purge away the dross from our life, to teach us to rely on Him alone. But our greatest redemption comes from our faith in the resurrection. Just as God the Father resurrected Jesus, so He will resurrect us. This — and not suffering — is the greatest fact for the Christian. There is no comparison between our present suffering and "the glory that is to be revealed to us."

Albert Schweitzer said once,

"Look back over those hours which passed over your life so calmly and contentedly. . . . If the whole of your life had been a succession of hours like those, do you know what would have become of you? You would [have] become selfish, hardhearted, lonely, without regard for higher things, for the pure, for God — and you would never have felt blessedness. When did it first dawn on you that we men don't live unto ourselves? When did the blessedness of compas-

sion bring comfort to you? In suffering. Where did
your heart come close to those who were so distant
and cold to you? In suffering. Where did you catch a
glimpse of the higher destiny of your life? In suffering. Where did you feel God was near to you? In
suffering. Where did you first realize the blessedness
of having a Father in heaven? In suffering.''

PRAYER

"My God, I have never thanked Thee for my thorn.
I have thanked Thee a thousand times for my
    roses,
but not once for my thorn.
I have been looking forward to a world where
I should get compensation for my crosses,
but I have never thought of the cross as itself
    a present glory.

Thou, Divine Love, whose human fact has been
perfected through sufferings,
teach me the value of my thorn . . .
and then shall I know that my tears
have made my rainbow, and I shall be
able to say, 'It was good for me that
I have been afflicted.' ''

—D. D. Matheson

TO KNOW GOD!
THAT'S LIFE!

Sunday of the Holy Fathers
of the First Ecumenical Council.
John 17:1-13.

Man needs to know. This is why he is impelled to go to the moon, to discover, to investigate, to conduct scientific research. There is so much to know in the universe. It has been said that all the knowledge of man from early history to 1845 equaled one inch. From 1845 to 1945 two inches. From 1945 until now the knowledge acquired equals the height of the Washington Monument. There has been an explosion in knowledge. The marvel of it all is that man not only can know what is in the universe; he can also come to know Him Who stands behind the universe: God.

The Apostle John writes in today's Gospel lesson, "And this is life eternal, that they may know Thee, the only true God, and Jesus Christ, whom Thou hast sent" (John 17:3). The supreme blessing of the human soul is that it can know God. The supreme tragedy is that often it does not want to know Him, being distracted by the things of this world. To know God is not just another kind of knowledge: it is a matter of life or death, heaven or hell.

The Catechism tells us that we were born for nothing else. We live for no other purpose than to know, love, and serve God on earth, and to enjoy Him for all eternity. To know God is the only real purpose of life. St. Anthony said once, "The most grievous loss and the greatest disaster is for a person not to know God."

One of the greatest universities in our land was founded on the principle that there is no higher knowledge than to know God. John Harvard left his library and half of his estate so that the college bearing his name might be established. This is what

103

he said in his bequest which resulted in the founding of Harvard University:

"Every student in this college shall be plainly instructed and earnestly pressed to consider the main ends of life and to know God and Jesus Christ, whom to know is eternal life." It was on the basis that there is nothing higher or more important than to know God in Christ that Harvard was founded.

We read in Jeremiah 9:23 - 24, "Let not the wise man glory in his wisdom, let not the mighty man glory in his might, let not the rich man glory in his riches; but let him who glories glory in this, that he understands and knows me, that I am the Lord who practices kindness, justice and righteousness in the earth; for in these I delight, says the Lord."

Despite the fantastic explosion of knowledge these past forty years man has yet to discover a source of wisdom that can pull all the pieces of life together. Such wisdom is to be found only in God.

Personal Knowledge

The purpose of all Christian preaching and teaching is to help us get to know God. I don't mean just to get to know *about* Him, but to get to *know* Him. There is a world of difference between knowing about someone and really knowing him.

We may know much about a famous person. Whatever he does receives wide publicity but very few people really know him as a person. Yet the whole world knows about him.

When the Bible talks about knowing God, it does not mean knowing certain ideas *about* Him, but knowing him *personally*. The word *know* in Hebrew means knowledge that comes from a close, personal relationship. "This is life eternal that they may know Thee — the only true God — and Jesus Christ Whom Thou hast sent." *"Know Thee,"* not *"about Thee."* Knowing *about* God or Christ does not save, does not give eternal life. Knowing Christ does.

The essence of Christianity is a direct personal encounter between two persons — ourselves and God. Man is called to establish an intimate, deeply personal I - Thou relationship with God. Of all creatures on earth only man was created with the capacity and ability to know God.

St. Athanasius wrote:

"For what use is existence to the creature if he cannot know his Maker? How could men be reasonable beings if they had no knowledge of the Word and Reason of the Father through Whom they had received their being? They would be no better than the beasts, had they no knowledge except of earthly things; and why should God have made them at all, if He had not intended them to know Him?"

There are many people today — important people — who give the impression that they have all of life figured out. But in reality they are just floating around in life. They are empty inside. They may know much about psychology or economics but they have no spiritual or heavenly certainty. They are saying and doing what society expects them to do and say. Outwardly they are giving the impression of confidence and direction, but inwardly they are filled with terrifying uncertainty. They can never say with absolute assurance where they will go when their life on earth is ended.

Mark Twain's child said to her father after the latter had been bragging about how many great and famous people in the world he knew, "Gee, dad, you know everybody except God."

Who Makes God Known?

Getting to know someone is difficult — very difficult — unless the other person chooses to open up and reveal himself to us. God has already done this in Christ. He has opened Himself up to us. This is why we Christians believe that it is impossible to know God apart from Christ. "No one has ever seen God; the only Son, who is in the bosom of the Father, he has made him known" (John 1:18). Only He who is in the bosom of the Father — in the closest possible relationship to Him — can make God known. This is why St. Paul said, "I decided to know nothing among you except Jesus Christ and Him crucified." It is only by Christ that we can come to know God not as a distant, remote, unapproachable deity, but as a Father and Friend who loves and cares personally and intimately.

105

Tools We Need to Discover God

The question is: how do we come to know God? As different tools are needed to investigate truth in the various sciences, i.e., a microscope in biology, a telescope in astronomy, etc., so we need entirely different tools in order to come to know God Who is Spirit and Truth. We need spiritual tools to understand spiritual things. For example:

1. We simply cannot know God without *purity of heart*. Jesus said, "Blessed are the pure in heart for they shall see God." One cannot come to know God without inner purity which is born of daily repentance. As St. John Climacus said, "Purity makes its disciple a theologian, who of himself grasps the dogmas of the Trinity."

2. In addition to purity of heart, we cannot know God *without the Holy Spirit*. "No one can say that Jesus is Lord without the Holy Spirit" (I Cor. 12:3). We can come to know God only through the Logos in the Holy Spirit. The Holy Spirit is God teaching us God. The Elder Silouan (Silvanus) who died on Mount Athos in 1938 wrote about knowing God through the Holy Spirit:

> *"We may study as much as we will, but we shall still not come to know the Lord unless we live according to His commandments, for the Lord is not made known through learning, but by the Holy Spirit. Many philosophers and scholars have arrived at a belief in the existence of God, but they have not come to know Him. To believe in God is one thing, to know God is another. Both in heaven and on earth the Lord is made known only by the Holy Spirit, and not through ordinary learning."* [1]

3. In addition to purity of heart and the Holy Spirit, we cannot know God apart from the Gospels. As Fr. Florovsky wrote, "God created man so that he would hear His words, receive them, grow in them, and through them become a participant of eternal life." Fr. Hopko writes, "There is an essen-

---

[1] "The Undistorted Image: Staretz Silouan" by Sofrony. Faith Press. London. 1958. pp. 115-118.

tial 'built in' condition in man, built in by God Himself (His image and likeness) which allows man truly to know God and to fulfill his existence through this very knowledge."[2]

4. In addition to purity of heart, the Holy Spirit and the Gospels, we cannot know God without *love*. The Apostle John wrote, "God is love, and he who abides in love abides in God, and God abides in Him" (I John 4:16). We know God by love, for He is pure love. Our knowledge of Him is rooted and expressed in love.

5. Purity of heart, the Holy Spirit, the Gospels, love and, fifth, *prayer*. We cannot know God without *prayer*. For to pray truly is to be a theologian; to pray truly is to know God and to be united with Him.

6. We cannot know God unless we are *in living communion with Him* and God is present within us. In the words of St. Gregory of Nyssa: "The Lord does not say that it is blessed to know something about God but to have God present within onself."[3] He goes on to say that the best way to know God is to be like Him.

7. Finally, we cannot know God without *obedience*. Matthew the Poor writes that the Gospel is spiritual and "must be obeyed and lived through the Holy Spirit before it can be understood. If anyone living outside the Gospel tries to understand it he will stumble and fall. . . . But if anyone has . . . total obedience to God . . . that person enters into the mystery of the Gospel without being aware of it."[4]

Thus the tools we need to know God are not the microscope or the telescope since God is not physical. The tools we need to know God are spiritual: purity of heart, the Holy Spirit, the Gospels, love, prayer, His inner presence, obedience, and a deep hunger and thirst for Him.

[2] "All the Fullness of God," T. Hopko. SVS Press. Crestwood, NY. 1982. p. 61.

[3] "Commentary on the Beatitudes," (Ancient Christian Writers 18); Paulist Press. Westminster, MD, (1954). p. 118.

[4] "The Communion of Love" by Matthew the Poor. SVS Press. Crestwood, NY. 1984. p. 20.

A Matter of Time

One cannot really know a person unless one is willing to spend time with him. Yet man's value system is so confused that he is willing to spend twenty years learning a vocation and not five minutes a day to know God. We go through life acquainted with almost everything except God. The result of this is described by F. J. Sheed:

"Not knowing God he (modern man) does not know what he is; equally he does not know what he is here for, where he is supposed to be going, how to get there. He is on a journey, but does not know his destination, has neither a map of the road nor the rules of the road. Lacking this indispensable knowledge, men occupy themselves with other matters, beer, or women or rare stamps or science. One man, for instance, is a great authority on butterflies. Upon his subject he will talk endlessly and with an admirable enthusiasm. But interrupt his discourse on butterflies to ask him what he knows about himself and where he is supposed to be going and how: he will answer that these are religious questions, and that he has no time for them, being so deeply engaged with his butterflies. The thing is farcical but terrifying. One can make no sense of a man who gives so much attention to butterflies that he has none left for his own meaning."[5]

What is there to say of a person who has all the time in the world to get to know butterflies, or electrical engineering, or restaurant management but none to get to know God and himself? Some people know a lot of things but they know nothing about what really matters. Let me ask you a deeply personal question at this point: how much time did you spend this past week trying to get to know God better?

A Matter of Study

Getting to know God is a matter of time but also a matter of study. D. T. Niles tells of meeting a man once who kept saying, "I do not believe that," when some subject connected with the Christian faith was raised. One day he said to this

---

[5] "Theology and Sanity" by F. J. Sheed. Sheed and Ward. New York. 1946. p. 333.

person, "Wait a minute 'til I get a piece of paper and a pencil and let me write down a list of all the things you do not believe." Before long he had compiled an imposing list. He did not believe that Jesus Christ was God become man. He did not believe that Jesus Christ worked any miracles. He did not believe that Jesus Christ died for our sins. He did not believe that Jesus Christ rose from the dead, and so on. When D. T. Niles had written all this down, he asked him, "When did you last read any of the Gospels?" He replied, "Not since I left Sunday School." Whereupon his friend tore into two the paper on which he had written down his list of unbeliefs and threw it into a wastepaper basket. He called him intellectually dishonest.

How much like many of us! We say we do not believe, but are not even willing to be fair enough to sit down and read the gospel record of the things we are denying. We can disbelieve if we want to, but let's at least be honest about it. Sit down and meet Jesus personally in the Gospels. Acquaint yourself personally with Him beyond the Sunday school level before you start denying Him.

Not Just Any God

Let me tell you about some people I meet who say to me, "It is important to believe in God, some god, just about any god," and then they often add, "We're all going to the same place, aren't we?"

I don't know about you, but for me it is not true that any god will do. I notice that it was not true for the Apostle John either. He said, "This is eternal life, to know You, the only true God, and Jesus Christ whom You have sent."

Get To Know Jesus

Getting to know Jesus makes everything come alive. If the liturgy seems stale, the sacraments empty rituals, the solution is to get to know Jesus. He will help you see that He is at the center of every liturgy and sacrament, offering Himself to you in love. If the Bible sounds more like bad news than good news, the solution is to get to know Jesus. You will find that the Bible is Christ speaking to you words of everlasting life. If you find coming to Church on Sunday a chore, the solution is to get to know Jesus personally. Then you will crave to be with Him. There is no substitute for getting to know Jesus personally and learning to love Him faithfully. When this happens, everything changes; everything comes alive.

What Does It Mean to Know Jesus?

To know God in Christ is to be set free. "You will know the truth and the truth will set you free" (John 8:32). Jesus is the Truth Who sets us free from the delusions of sin. To know God in Christ is to know that He knows you and loves you. To know God in Christ is to love. "He who does not love does not know God," writes the Apostle John, "For God is love." C. H. Dodd said, "To know God is to experience His love in Christ and to return that love in obedience." To know God in Christ is to experience the new creation. Asked what he knew about God one Christian said, "Not much, but what I know has changed my life." To know God in Christ is to know ourselves, our purpose in life, the essence of our being. To know God is to live — really live the life of God in the here and now. "This is life, to know Thee . . . and Jesus Christ . . ." No other knowledge saves. No other knowledge leads to eternal life. It is not what you know but who you know that leads to eternal life.

What Difference Does It Make?

To know God in Christ is to be able to respond to life with the assurance of "I know" as did St. Paul. Paul did not entrust his life to an "unknown God" or to a vague "Man Upstairs" or to somebody he did not know. When sin beset him he said, "*I know* whom I have believed, and am persuaded that he is able to keep that which I have committed unto him against that day" (2 Timothy 1:12). When trouble pressed in on him he said, "*We know* that all things work together for good to those who love God" (Romans 8:28). When death drew near he said, "*We know* that if the earthly tent we live in is destroyed, we have a building from God, a house not made with hands, eternal in the heavens" (II Corinthians 5:1).

A certain mother said about her child:

110

"When my children were small, my younger son Brian was afraid to go into a swimming pool unless I went with him. I couldn't understand why he was so timid.

'Why do I have to be with you?' I said to him one day. 'The lifeguard is right there. Don't you know that if you get into trouble, he'll save you much quicker than I?'

'But I don't *know* him, mommy.' Brian answered, clinging to my hand.

"And so I took Brian and introduced him to the lifeguard. The two of them talked, and somehow that gave Brian the security he needed to swim without me."

There are people who hesitate to turn to Jesus because they don't know Him. If they did, they would trust Him with their lives. They would find in Him life's greatest peace and security and would be able to say with the Apostle John: *"This is life . . .* to know Thee the only true God and Jesus Christ whom Thou hast sent."

PRAYER

Dear Lord, You have been with us for so many years and yet we do not know You. What we know about you is nothing compared to what remains to be known if we will give You our time, our obedience, our love, our faith. Help us to know You personally, for to know You is to live. Amen.

111

PENTECOST - A
RELIGION OF POWER
The Feast of Pentecost.
John 7:37 - 8:12.

Pentecost — a day when there were strange happenings in Jerusalem, a sudden, mighty rush of wind, tongues of fire, a Babel of strange languages, Pentecost, the birthday of the Church — when a company of unlearned, fearful disciples, waiting for the promised gift of the Holy Spirit, suddenly received that promise and were changed into learned, enthusiastic, active witnesses for Christ, confident in their faith and their future.

Pentecost — what does it mean to us? Where shall we look today for results like those that followed that first great breakthrough of the Spirit?

What did that event mean to those who experienced it?

Forty days after Easter our Lord ascended into heaven. One can imagine how lonely and insecure the apostles must have felt when they saw their Master leave them. Before He left, however, He promised that He would not leave them alone. He would send the Paraclete, the Comforter, the third person of the Godhead — the Holy Spirit — to guide them, strengthen them, comfort them, and remain with them until the end of time.

An Amazing Experience

Then just ten days later, came Pentecost — an amazing experience. One can almost hear the disciples exclaiming: "Why it's true! This is what the Master promised and it's happening. Our fears are gone. We feel within us the upsurge of new power, new wisdom, a new knowledge of languages we never before understood. God is here with us now!"

The results were that Peter, once so fearful that he denied he ever knew Jesus, now stands up before thousands of people and proclaims with conviction that Jesus is the Son of God. He tells his hearers to repent and be baptized and they do — three thousand of them become Christians as a result of Peter's sermon on Pentecost.

Pentecost, the day the Spirit of God broke through to the disciples and led them from discouragement to confidence, from paralysis to creative living, from worry about their own problems to a vision of God active in the world.

St. Basil says of the meaning of Pentecost:

"Through the Holy Spirit our return to paradise is achieved, we are elevated to the heavenly kingdom, and become once more the children of God. Through Him we are able to call God, Father; we are able to become partakers of the grace of Jesus Christ, to be called children of light, and to share in everlasting glory . . ." (On the Holy Spirit, ch. 15).

God Is Here Now

If Pentecost means anything, it means, "GOD IS HERE NOW!" He is not only the God of the great yesterday, Who created the world and sent the prophets; not only the God of the great tomorrow, of the eternal world and eternal life; He is also the God of the great today. The Holy Spirit is the Present tense of God: *God with us now.*

He is called Spirit because He is like the breath of God which fills us with God's life and power. As Spirit He is like the air we breathe, which surrounds us, is nearest us, outside us and within us and gives us life. The coming of the Holy Spirit, the holy breath of God, is Pentecost.

Pentecost did not happen just once. It happens today. It can happen to you. Who is it who does not need the inner strength which the Spirit of God alone can impart? Who is it who does not need the insight and the right word to heal a broken relationship? Is not one of the chief characteristics of modern man the fact that he cannot stand up under pressure? Although he appears to be strong on the outside, man is so weak on the inside that even the little setbacks in life knock his inner world to pieces?

114

"House Power"

Among electricians there is what is known as "house power." Frequently we see newspaper ads asking the question: Is your house supplied with enough power to run all the appliances you need for adequate living? If not, then you are constantly blowing fuses when too heavy a load is laid upon the "house power." The same thing happens in our personal lives. Think of the heavy demands that are made on our "personal power" every day. Think of the power we need to face the many problems and temptations of life. Think of the inner strength we need to cope with the pressures of everyday living. When we do not have sufficient inner power, we blow fuses—"blow our tops." We go to pieces emotionally. It is a sign of frustration, of inadequacy to face the demands of living.

The Great Breakthrough

It was the Spirit of God breaking through at Pentecost that gave the disciples the inner power and wisdom to face and withstand all outside pressures victoriously.

This same Holy Spirit is available to us today through the Church, through prayer, through the sacraments.

"You shall receive power, when the Holy Spirit comes to you," promised Christ.

St. John Chrysostom in his homily on the Feast of Pentecost says:

"The all gracious God today bestowed upon us gifts, too great to be adequately expressed in words. Therefore, let us all rejoice together, and while rejoicing, let us praise our God. . . . For I ask, what was given to us for our salvation that was not given to us by the Holy Spirit? He freed us from slavery, adopted and called us to the freedom of the children of God. From this fountain (i.e. the Holy Spirit) flow prophecies, the grace of healing, and all the other gifts and fruits with which the Church is wont to adorn herself."

Running Out of Gas

Someone related an experience he had while driving through the countryside with his family one spring day. They were enjoying all the beauty around them: the wild flowers in the fields, the budding trees, and the shimmering lake. Suddenly the driver looked at the gas gauge, and saw that the indicator was on the empty mark. He said, "Before that I enjoyed all the beauty around me, but then when I noticed that I might not have enough gas to get to the next gas station, I couldn't enjoy any of the beauty around me at all. Not a single thing could take my mind away from the possibility of our running out of gas."

So it is in life. One of our great fears is that of running out of gas, running out of power. So long as we are sure that power is available, that we are not "running out of gas," we can enjoy life and all the wonderful things God has made possible for us. But there is nothing worse than to go through life feeling that at any moment we may run out of power.

Man was made to run on only one type of fuel: the Holy Spirit. Only He provides the kind of power and direction we need. We may try to use other types of fuel but they will never give us the same mileage, the same dependability, the same sustaining power. Just as a car breaks down if we try to make it run on Channel No. 5 instead of gas because it smells better, so man breaks down if he tries to make himself run on anything but the Holy Spirit. "Do you not know that your bodies are temples of the Holy Spirit?" asks Paul. He is our sustaining power.

No worse advice can be given to some people than to say, "Try! Try harder!" A person who suffers from chronic fatigue or strain, or one who has experienced shock, cannot try harder. He has already tried too hard. What he needs is not more effort but more resources, not more pressure on the accelerator but more gas in the tank, more power. What he needs is God, the Holy Spirit. "Ye shall receive power after the Holy Spirit is come upon you."

The Ultimate Purpose is Fulfilled

Before Jesus ascended into heaven, He said, *"It is better for you that I go away because then the Holy Spirit will come to you."* Imagine! Jesus Himself telling us that it is better that He go away because then He can send us the Holy Spirit! Pentecost is the ultimate purpose for which Christ became man and came to earth. For, having been redeemed, washed and purified by the blood of Christ, we were made fit by Jesus to receive the Holy Spirit. On Pentecost He — the Spirit of God — came to fill the Church with His presence. The purpose for which Jesus came was accomplished. *God the Spirit now abides in us 'til the end of time.*

Pentecost Came for Stephen, Peter and Paul

Pentecost came for St. Stephen, one of the first deacons. He spoke with such power that the enemies of Christ were stirred up. He was arrested. When given the opportunity to present the story of Christ, he did so with such eloquence and conviction that the people were stirred up. They gnashed on him with their teeth. "But he, *being full of the Holy Spirit,* looked up steadfastly into heaven, and saw the glory of God, and Jesus standing on the right hand of God." Later they cast him out of the city and stoned him. As he was dying, he prayed, "Lord, lay not this sin to their charge." For St. Stephen, Pentecost had come. Full of the Holy Spirit, he was able to forgive his murderers.

Pentecost came for St. Stephen. It came for the apostles. What a difference it made when on Pentecost the Holy Spirit came to them! They went forth to live courageous and victorious lives. Peter, the weakling, who had deserted the Lord in His moment of utmost need — all of a sudden becomes a bold preacher of the Word! Saul of Tarsus, the great persecutor of Christians, makes a complete about face on the road to Damascus and sets out to turn the world upside down for Christ. "You shall receive power," Christ promised, "when the Holy Spirit comes to you." The apostles received that power.

Power Today

So can we. Power to turn the barrenness of the soul into a garden of beauty; power to resist the onslaught of sin — or, having fallen into sin, to tread the path of the prodigal back to the Father's house and be assured of full and free forgiveness; power to bear the burdens of each day; power to break the chains of sinful habits that have long enslaved us; power to outlast the storm; power to stand up for that which is right; power to forgive, to love, to achieve the final victory.

The stichera of the Great Vespers Service of Pentecost praise the Holy Spirit with these words:

"The Holy Spirit is the giver of all gifts. He pours forth prophecies, perfects the priesthood, teaches wisdom to the illiterate, and transforms fishermen into theologians; He brings together into one community the entire Church of God. O Comforter, one with the Father in nature and co-reigning with Him, glory to You."

"You shall receive power when the Holy Spirit comes to you . . ." "He who believes in me," said Jesus in today's Gospel lesson, "out of his heart flow rivers of living water. Now this He said about the Spirit, which those who believe in Him were to receive." In a few moments we shall kneel to pray that this same Holy Spirit may come to us on this day of Pentecost as He came to the apostles 2,000 years ago to replace our barrenness with beauty, our weakness with power, our emptiness with the fullness of God's presence.

St. Symeon the NEW THEOLOGIAN prayed:

"Come, true light;
Come, eternal life;
Come, hidden mystery;
Come, treasure without name; . . .
Come, incessant joy!
Come, light unfading;
Come, hope which will save all.
Come, resurrection of the dead;
Come, O powerful one, who fulfillest,
transformest and changest all things
by Thy will alone;
Come, garland never withered; . . .
Come, breath of my own life, consolation of
my lowly heart."

Come, Spirit of God, fill us with God's presence.
Come, make our bodies temples of God.

Come, fill us with power to overcome.
Come, restore the image of God in us.
Come, strengthen our faith.
Come, empower us to speak and work for You
    in the world.
Come, forgive our sins.
Come, breathe into us the life of God, immortal,
    everlasting.
Come, Holy Spirit.
Come! As the fallow earth craves rain,
    we crave You.

CONFESSING CHRIST
BEFORE THE WORLD
The Sunday of All Saints.
Matthew 10:32-33, 37, 38 and 19:27-30.

The first Sunday after Pentecost is dedicated to the memory of all saints and martyrs — known and unknown — throughout history. Called the Sunday of All Saints, it shows that there is a direct connection between last Sunday — Pentecost — and today, All Saints Day. For, one of the purposes of the coming of the Holy Spirit on Pentecost was to produce saints.

Sainthood is not an exceptional or abnormal state of Christian holiness reserved for a select few. Sainthood is the normal flowering of every Christian's life in the Trinity. We are all called to be saints. In fact, in the New Testament Church the word "saint" and "Christian" were interchangeable. Jesus addressed all people without exception when He said, "Therefore, be perfect as your heavenly Father is perfect" (Matthew 5:48). St. Paul also reminds us of our duty to pursue holiness. "This is the will of God — your sanctification" (I Cor. 4:3). A saint is not someone who is perfect. He is merely a forgiven sinner who follows Jesus.

Speaking in a sermon on the first Sunday after the descent of the Holy Spirit, Deacon Constantine (6th century) of Constantinople said, "The Greek Church, by a distinguished and very illustrious feast, honors the memory of those immortal flowers which the whole earth brings forth from that soil which is continuously refreshed by the flowering streams of the Holy Spirit."

The Epistle lesson today describes the sufferings of the saints — prophets and martyrs — who through the ages were stoned, put to the sword and tortured "of whom the world was not worthy.'

121

The Conditions of Sainthood

The Gospel lesson for this Sunday is a collection of sayings by Jesus wherein He lays down the conditions of holiness.

The first condition for sainthood: "Everyone who acknowledges me before men, I will acknowledge before my Father who is in heaven . . ."

The second condition for sainthood: "He who loves father or mother more than me is not worthy of me."

The third condition for sainthood: "He who does not take up his cross and follow after me is not worthy of me."

The fourth condition of sainthood: "Everyone who has forsaken houses, or brethren, or sisters, or father, or mother, or wife, or children, or lands, for my name's sake, shall receive a hundredfold and shall inherit eternal life."

No Silent Witness

Today we shall concentrate on the first condition for Christian holiness: confessing or acknowledging Christ before the world. Acknowledging Christ before men is one of the fruits of the Holy Spirit in us. One of the first things Peter did after Pentecost was to stand up publicly and acknowledge Christ. If we are true Christians and the Spirit indeed abides in us, every one of us will be acknowledging Christ before the world by what we say, by what we do, and by what we are.

Christianity grew because Christ's followers were not silent. The apostles said, "We cannot but speak of the things we have seen and heard." In expressing their faith, the early Christians stormed against the evils of their day until the foundations of the decadent Roman Empire began to crumble.

One of Christ's great commands to us was, "Let your light so shine before men . . ." We are hardly followers of Jesus if it is not obvious to those around us whose side we are on. Gabriel Marcel said once, "I am obliged to bear witness because I hold, as it were, a particle of light, and to keep it to myself would be equivalent to extinguishing it."

Equipped For the Task

The purpose of the Sacrament of Confirmation or Chrismation which is administered to Orthodox Christians at baptism is to make Pentecost personal to us. We are given the Holy Spirit, as were the apostles at Pentecost, to equip us for the task of acknowledging and confessing Christ's name before the world. We are especially anointed for this task.

Acknowledging Christ before men is not something for which you need a theological education. As D. T. Niles said, "It is one beggar telling another beggar where he found bread. We do not need to badger or hound people. We simply share the story of what Jesus Christ has done for us." This is the meaning of the Greek word "martus": to share with others what we have seen and experienced. This is exactly what the Samaritan woman did after she met Jesus at the well. She ran back home and told her townspeople about what Jesus had told her.

One Ant to Another

A missionary to Africa watched a black ant crawl up a table leg and onto the table to some sugar that had been spilled there. It ate its desire, crawled back down the table leg, and disappeared. Soon two more black ants crawled up the table leg to the spilled sugar. They ate and left. Moments later there was a steady stream of black ants crawling up the table leg, for the sugar. One had to surmise that through their communication system, one ant had communicated to others and said, "I have found something good, and I want to share it with you." Is not this what acknowledging Christ before the world is all about?

No Active Orthodox Witness

Yet how many of us today are willing to say a good word for Jesus? This is particularly true of us Orthodox Christians. Fr. Theodore Bobosh published a study of converts to the Orthodox Church and discovered that one of the main complaints of those who found their way to our Church was that there was no active Orthodox witness. Let me quote what some of them said:

"There was no active Orthodox witness to attract me to the Church. I somehow found my own way in."

"I never came into contact with any Orthodox witness."

123

"The indifference to the Faith on the part of so many 'born Orthodox' is appalling. Many even of the clergy don't realize the need for an Orthodox witness and mission and would be just as happy if there weren't any."

"My greatest sorrow is that we seem to have almost no need, no urge, to proclaim salvation."

"Evangelism, evangelism, evangelism — we have the greatest gift of all, why are we so reticent about sharing it?" [1]

Hiding Our Faith

If that well-known question were asked of us: "If you were on trial for being a Christian, would there be enough evidence to convict you?," I'm afraid that for many of us there would be little or no evidence to convict us as Christians.

We are like that young Christian person who went to work one summer in a lumber camp. Some of his friends told him that the tough lumbermen would make life miserable for him because of his Christian faith. Bravely he went and spent the summer. When he came home his friends asked him if the men had laughed at him for being a Christian. He said, "No, they didn't laugh at me because of my being a Christian. They never found out."

The Persecution of Saints Today

Contrast this with the early Christian saints and martyrs whom we honor today. Millions of them during the early centuries were brought before Roman magistrates to be questioned about their faith. If they responded by confessing that they were Christians, they were thrown into prison. Every means — human and inhuman — was used to try to force them to renounce Christ. Those who did not were thrown to the beasts or roasted alive. Part of the remains of these early martyrs are usually imbedded in the altar tables of our churches when they are consecrated.

---

[1] *"Come and See: Encouraging the Orthodox Church,"* Theo. Bobosh, Editor. *DRE-OCA. Syosset, NY. 1983. pp. 8, 13, 27, 46, 97.*

124

The persecution of Christians has not stopped. It continues today in many countries, notably the Soviet Union. Listen to this description of Orthodox Christians today suffering for refusing to deny their faith; suffering for acknowledging and confessing Christ before the world:

"The author describes the arrival of Easter in late April . . . but Siberia held its winter savagely. On Easter Day itself a group of women from Voronezh, imprisoned for their Orthodox faith, asked to be dispensed from work that day. The camp officials ordered them out to do their slave labor in the forest regardless, and they were driven by the rifle butts of the guards. When they arrived at the clearing where they were to do their logging, they dropped their axes and saws, sat down on the tree trunks and began to sing the Easter liturgy. The guards rounded them up, marched them out onto the ice covering one of the pools in the forest, and made them take their boots off. Barefoot, they stood their ground on the ice and recited every syllable of the liturgy, while the other prisoners besought the guards not to be so brutal to these harmless people." [2]

These are Christians today who are suffering in Siberian prison camps for acknowledging and confessing Christ.

How One Person Acknowledged Jesus

May I conclude with this beautiful story of how one Christian acknowledged and confessed Christ to a stranger.

"For seven weeks Jerry and I went each morning for his cobalt treatments. I was quiet, but Jerry talked with everyone in the waiting room, encouraging them, sharing with them and on occasion even laughing heartily.

"One day I noticed a woman in a wheelchair, and from somewhere came the desire to speak with her. She barely acknowledged my presence. Although

[2] "Risen Indeed: Lessons In Faith from the USSR," M. Bourdeaux. SVS Press. Crestwood, NY. 1983. p. 88.

125

I was a bit perplexed, her lack of response seemed to trigger a question within me and I asked her, 'Do you know how much God loves you?'

"She shook her head. I knelt by her side and began to tell her about His love.

" 'I don't believe,' she murmured, as she turned her face away.

"That night I prayed for Wilma and asked God to show me a way to reach her. Very gently came the response: 'Don't take her anything of a religious nature. Take the handmade shawl in the top of your closet and wrap it around her, telling her that it really isn't a shawl at all but My arms, enfolding her in My love.'

"The next day I placed the shawl around Wilma's shoulders and explained where it had come from and why. She touhced it wonderingly and sat quiet for a moment. Then she raised her eyes to mine, and through her tears she whispered, 'I do believe, and may God bless you.' "

Jesus says, "Everyone who acknowledges me before men, *I will acknowledge before my Father who is in heaven."* Imagine Jesus placing His arms around you one day and acknowledging you before all the angels of heaven as His very own. That is what He says He will do. He will deny those who have denied Him and acknowledge those who have acknowledged Him before His Father in heaven. That means you and me!

PRAYER

Is there anyone greater than You, Lord?
Anyone more loving?
Anyone more forgiving?
Anyone more powerful?
Anyone more caring?
Why should I hesitate to acknowledge You,
to share You with others who are
hungering and thirsting and dying?
Grant me Your Holy Spirit that I may
praise You, acknowledge You and confess You
With every breath I draw. Amen.

MODERN DISCIPLES
The Calling of the Disciples.
Matthew 4:18 - 23.

The Gospel lesson today tells how Jesus called His disciples. "And He said to them, 'Follow me, and I will make you fishers of men.'"

Jesus directs these same words, "Follow me" to every Christian today. But how are we to follow Him in today's confused world?

Let us examine briefly how some other modern disciples have followed Jesus in the hope that their example may inspire us and shed some light on how we may follow Him in today's world.

A Disciple in Kwai Valley

During the Second World War a company of British soldiers was taken prisoner by the Japanese and sent to the Kwai Valley to build a railroad bridge. For a long time the prisoners lived in a state of hatred and resentment. They were mean and ugly to each other. They lived like animals, stealing food from each other and letting the starving die. Christianity had no part in their lives. One day a Japanese officer lined up the men and reported that a shovel was missing. The guilty man was to step forward and admit his guilt of stealing it. No one stepped forward. Then the officer threatened to shoot all of them if the guilty one did not speak up. There was no response. The officer again threatened violence. Then one man stepped forward. The rest were dismissed and the prisoner was taken away and beaten to death. A few days later it was learned that there was no missing shovel. Somebody had apparently counted wrong. Then the other prisoners realized that the man who stepped forward died to save their lives. This caused the whole atmosphere in the prison camp to change. Now they began to love and care for each other. Christianity began to mean something to them.

Many turned to Christ and started reading the Bible. One man decided to give his life to Christ by entering the ministry.

It all started when one man decided to follow Christ in a particular situation by giving his life to save his comrades: "Greater love has no man than to give his life for his friends."

A Disciple in Colorado

Mrs. Margaret Rossi, a devout Christian, lives in a small town in Colorado where more than 26% of all persons are over 65. The nearest doctor or hospital is 21 miles away. Several aged persons, not being able to make the trip, stayed at home when in dire need of medical help. In many cases these lonely old sick people would die for lack of medical help and it was several days before their bodies were discovered in their homes. To meet this need, Mrs. Rossi organized the Friendly Visitors and Transportation Service consisting of volunteers whom she directs. They call at least once a week on the old people who live alone. Many of them are confined to a wheelchair, have severe arthritis, diabetes or other physical problems. The regularity of visits is important, because "when old people know that someone is coming, it gives them something to look forward to," Mrs. Rossi says. In many instances, the Friendly Visitors also make daily telephone calls to the aged. The lives of these formerly forsaken and lonely persons have all changed because one person, Mrs. Rossi, decided to follow Christ and make real His love for the aged and the infirm: "I was sick and you visited me."

A Disciple in Africa

An African woman was brought to a rural clinic in Southern Rhodesia. She was desperately ill with an extremely severe case of syphilis complicated by other illnesses which she in her weakness could not throw off. Her only safeguard against the insanity caused by syphilis was in recurring attacks of malaria whose extremely high fever burned out the syphilis germs before they could cause major damage in the brain. An outcast from her village, a rejected plaything of dissolute men, she was afraid and hostile when she was brought to the clinic. She was withdrawn; never speaking to anyone. Slowly she began to respond to all the loving care she was receiving. One day as the missionary nurse cared for her, she suddenly burst out crying, slipped to the floor, kissed the feet of the nurse, and sobbed out her question why anybody should treat her with such loving-kindness.

The nurse sat beside her and held her shaking shoulders until the wild sobbing ceased. Then she told of the Christ Who walked by Galilee, how He loved people who had suffered, how He cleansed them of their sins and healed them of their diseases. The nurse told how Christ had come to her when she was a young girl in Europe and asked her to go to Africa, there to bring His love and healing to those who needed it. She went on to say that, best of all, she did not come to Africa alone, but that Christ was there, too, and that He, at that moment, was seeking to come into that African woman's heart to cleanse her from her sins and show her the fullness of His love. When that African woman left that clinic she was a radiantly different person, healed by Christ in spirit as well as in body. She married and established a Christian home that has been a center of joy and peace in her village. All because one Christian nurse chose to follow Christ when He called her to serve Him in Africa.

A Disciple in Philadelphia

Naval Reserve Airman James R. George, age 23, from Georgia, was on leave in Philadelphia and intent on seeing the historical sights of that city. In a subway station that evening he was suddenly confronted with a sight he hadn't expected to see. A gang of young hoodlums had cornered a young girl and were about to attack her. At the other end of the platform six men waiting for the subway train, were just watching, making no effort to intervene. George called to them to help him save the girl who was screaming. But they shrugged their shoulders and would not pay any attention. It was no business of theirs.

But this young Christian boy threw off his jacket and sailed all by himself into that vicious gang of punks. He threw them right and left, sent them sprawling all over the platform. They came back at him, and beat him up, leaving him unconscious. But the commotion attracted the attention of the subway teller who called the police. The hoodlums ran off; the girl was saved. Naval Reserve Airman James R. George, reared in a Christian home, chose to heed the call of Christ that came to him in that moment of need. He came to the rescue of one of God's defenseless children. The mayor of Philadelphia presented him with a citation and commended him for his bravery.

A Disciple in Atlanta

One final example. It was 7:30 in the morning in Atlanta, Georgia. The telephone rang in the home of a man named Jack Stevens. It was the voice of a friend saying, "Jack, I promised to take a poor little mother and her four-year-old son to the hospital at eight o'clock. They have to go right away. This little boy is in the last stages of leukemia. We have to get him to the hospital fast. But my car won't start. Will you take them to the hospital for me?"

Jack agreed. He went at once and put the mother in the front seat. The frail emaciated little boy was so weak that he couldn't sit up. His mother held him in her arms. As he sat there, the little boy looked at Mr. Stevens with his big lustrous eyes and asked, "Are you God?"

Stevens was startled, "No, son, why do you ask?"

"Because my mother told me God was coming to take me to a beautiful place," the child replied.

Stevens was shaken. "Son, I am going to take you to a beautiful place, a place where kind people will love you and take care of you and be good to you."

Four days later the little boy did go to a beautiful place on the wings of God. But Stevens could not get that little face and the question "Are you God?" out of his mind. He decided then and there: "I am going to devote my life to working for God." He consecrated himself to a lifetime career in youth and guidance welfare work. Like the disciples in today's Gospel lesson, he left everything and followed Christ.

We are not God — any of us — but we are a part of God, members of His Body — the Church. When we follow Jesus and consecrate our life to Him as did the original twelve disciples and as do countless modern disciples like the prisoner of Kwai, Mrs. Margaret Rossi of Colorado, the missionary nurse in

130

Rhodesia, Naval Reserve Airman James R. George in Philadelphia and Jack Stevens in Atlanta — when we follow Jesus as these people did, something wonderful happens. We begin to feel the presence of God among us. No wonder that little sick boy asked Mr. Stevens, "Are you God?"

PRESCRIPTION FOR WORRY
The Third Sunday of Matthew.
Matthew 6:22-33.

"Your wife used to be so nervous. Now she seems quite cured. How come?"

The husband replied, "She is cured. The doctor told her that nervousness was a sign of old age."

"Worry is the advance interest you pay on troubles that seldom come," it has been said.

The world has so many problems. If Moses came down from Mt. Sinai today, the tablets he carried would be two aspirins.

Studies have shown that worry can cause glaucoma, hysterical blindness, tooth decay, high blood pressure, colitis, diabetes, heart trouble, circulatory ailments and asthma.

No wonder Jesus speaks about worry in today's Gospel lesson. Let's say some basic things about how to face this great problem that we all encounter.

Worry About the Things You Can Change

First, there is great widsom in knowing which things to worry about. In other words, don't worry about what you cannot possibly change. Worry about the things you can change. Someone wrote:

You cannot control how long you will live, but you can control how widely and deeply you will live.

You cannot control the shape of your face, but you can control its expression.

You cannot control the other fellow's opportunities, but you can grasp your own.

You cannot control the weather, but you can control the moral atmosphere which surrounds you; you can control the weather within you.

You cannot control the distance that your head shall be above the ground, but you can control the height of the contents of your head.

You cannot control the other fellow's faults, but you can see to it that you yourself do not develop irritating habits.

Why worry about things you cannot control? Why not get busy and control the things that depend on you?

Don't Play God

The second major source of worry is when we try to play God. Don't ever try it. You cannot possibly do God's work. Only He can.

Someone has said, "I'm glad I am not bound
To make the world go round —
But only to discover and to do
With cheerful heart
The work that God appoints."

— Author unknown

Several people were talking about the cares and worries connected with their work. One man said that sometimes his worries piled up so much he thought he would break under the strain. But his friend replied, "That won't ever happen if you carry only your own share, and don't try to take God's work out of His hands!"

I shall never forget the story of the man who said how much better he felt after he resigned his position as general manager of the universe.

A true Christian is a person who knows what he can do and does it. But he also has a peace-bestowing humility in that he knows what he cannot do. And what he cannot do, he leaves in the capable hands of the only One Who can: a loving and all-powerful God.

Prayer

The third and last cure for worry that we shall discuss is trust and prayer.

134

"Look at the birds of the air: they neither sow nor reap nor gather into barns, and yet your heavenly Father feeds them. Are you not of more value than they? . . . Consider the lilies of the field, how they grow; they neither toil nor spin; yet I tell you, even Solomon in all his glory was not arrayed like one of these. But if God so clothes the grass of the field, which today is alive and tomorrow is thrown into the oven, will He not much more clothe you, O men of little faith?" If God so clothes the flowers—how much more YOU!

St. Paul echoes Jesus when he writes in Phil. 4:6-7, "Have no anxiety about anything." Like Jesus, he does not stop there. He goes on to give us the secret of the defeat of worry: ". . . but in everything by prayer and supplication with thanksgiving let your requests be made known to God. And the peace of God, which passes all understanding, will keep your hearts and your minds in Christ Jesus." *Bring it to God,* he says. *Always, in everything!* Bring it to God! You can talk to God about absolutely anything . . . anything whatever that is burdening your secret soul in the absolute knowledge and trust that He cares and is able to help.

Spread It Before the Lord

In the Old Testament Hezekiah received a disturbing letter from his enemy. It was the kind of letter to cause a person to lose his sleep for nights. But, Hezekiah having read the letter, "went up into the house of the Lord, and spread it before the Lord." Whatever the invading anxiety or worry is, we can always "spread it out" before the Lord in prayer.

"Let not your hearts be troubled," says Jesus. And He goes on to give us the secret of a worry-free heart. *"Believe* in God, *believe* also in me." Trust Him completely. Spread it all out before Him in prayer.

Dietrich Bonhoeffer, the German theologian, was in prison at the time of the Second World War in Hitler's Germany and was separated from his loved ones until the time of his execution. He was no stranger to worry. But through Christ he learned to overcome it. He wrote, "From the moment we wake until we fall asleep we must commend our loved ones wholly and unreservedly to God and leave them in His hands, trans-

forming our anxiety for them into prayers on their behalf"
(Letters and Papers from Prison). The result of such trust is "the
peace of God which passes all human understanding."

So, why worry about things you cannot change when there
are so many things you can change? Why worry as if you were
general manager of the universe? Thank God you're not. Don't
even try. Why worry when you can pray?

Why Worry When You Can Pray?

Worry? Why worry? *What can worry do?*
It never keeps a trouble from overtaking you.
It gives you indigestion and sleepless hours
*   at night.*
And fills with gloom the day, however fair and
*   bright.*

It puts a frown upon the face, and sharpness to
*   the tone.*
We're unfit to live with others and unfit to live
*   alone.*
Worry? Why worry? What can worry do?
It never keeps a trouble from overtaking you.

Pray? Why pray? *What can praying do?*
Praying really changes things, arranges life anew.
It's good for your digestion, gives peaceful sleep
*   at night.*
And fills the grayest, gloomiest day—with rays
*   of glowing light.*

It puts a smile upon your face, the love note in
*   your tone—*
Makes you fit to live with others, and fit to live
*   alone.*
Pray? Why pray? What can praying do?
It brings God down from heaven, to live and work
*   with you.*

—*Charles L. Allen*

WHO CARES?

The Feast of the Twelve Apostles.
Matthew 9:36 - 10:8.

A student in a huge university flunks out. Who cares? A white collar worker in a towering building goes bankrupt. Who cares? A punch press operator in a sprawling factory (a nameless number for both union and management) dies in a traffic accident. Who cares? A tenant in a modern high rise apartment commits suicide. Who cares? A senior citizen languishes alone in a nursing home. Who cares?

Depersonalization, estrangement, isolation, the lonely crowd—these are terms that characterize our age. In desperation a young girl cried out, "I can't bear it any longer. I am so depressed. I don't care whether I live or die. No one cares about me—I am all alone." Silently the great majority of people cry out for someone who will listen, who will understand, who will care.

God Cares

In the darkness of that despair and the question, "Who cares?" there is a positive answer: God cares. Christians care. The Church cares.

First, God cares. See how much He cares in the Gospel lesson today. We read, "When He (Jesus) saw the crowds, He had compassion for them, because they were harassed and helpless, like sheep without a shepherd" (Matt. 9:36). He cared so much that "he called to Him his twelve disciples and gave them authority over unclean spirits, to cast them out, and to heal every disease and every infirmity" (Matt. 10:1). He charged them to go and "heal the sick, raise the dead, cleanse lepers, cast out demons" (Matt. 10:8).

God cares. He cares for each one of us as if there were only one of us in the universe. He loved us and cared for us so much that he "gave his only son so that whoever believes in

137

him should not perish but have eternal life" (John 3:15). Each one of us is in God's intensive care unit. The very hairs of our head are numbered and known to Him. He cares. And because He cares, He promises in Isaiah 43:2, "When you pass through the waters, I will be with you; and through the rivers, they will not overflow you. When you walk through the fire, you will not be scorched, nor will the flame burn you."

Does God Care?

God cares, and because He cares, He does not play dice with the universe. He treats us as His beloved children.

A grief-stricken father said to his pastor one day, "Day before yesterday you buried my son. He was all we had. My heart lies buried out there with the body of my boy: and I am not interested in your opinions, your hopes, or your beliefs. I want to know whether or not you know anything about God. Does He care? Does it make any difference to Him that my boy is dead? Tell me — on your honor! *What do you know?*"

Then it was that "we beheld his glory," for that pastor in a voice that was strangely calm in spite of its intensity, answered the stricken father: "I will tell you what *I know. I know He cares!*"

"How do you know it?" the father asked.

"Because He lost an only son, Himself, once. He watched Him die upon a cross, innocent of any evil. *He knows what it is to lose an only son!*"

God cares!

Christians Care

Because He cares, He calls on us to care for the "people for whom Christ died." This is brought out in the liturgy where we are called upon to care for the universe and God's people. The Great litany mentions all sorts of people for whom God wants us to care. In the liturgy of St. Basil, we hold up to God in prayer almost everyone in the universe, even the miner who works in the depths of the earth. We are called to be God's caring people. "When one member suffers, all the members suffer with it" (I Cor. 12:26) was said of the church. If we do not feel this, we are not within the church.

I agree with the psychiatrist who said, "At all times in our lives we must have at least one person who cares about us and for whom we care ourselves. If we do not have this one caring person, we will not be able to fulfill our basic needs."

I like these words by Harold Ivan Smith:

> *"Even a boxer is guaranteed*
> > *someone*
> > *to stand in his corner*
> > *between rounds of brutal blows*
> *Someone to care for his needs*
> > *before the bell would summon*
> > *to yet another round.*
> *How many pilgrims*
> > *have struggled to their corner*
> > *only to be alone?*
> *Are we not to step between the ropes*
> > *to wipe a forehead or*
> > *to offer a word of encouragement?*
> *To risk the stain of sweat*
> > *the sting of blood*
> > *the despair of agony?*

The Rejected Dolphin

Jacques Cousteau relates the story of the strange behavior of a dolphin sighted near Corsica. The dolphin was not swimming but just watching the boat. They decided the dolphin was sick so they netted and examined it. The animal showed no sign of fear. There was no sign of a wound. They injected a stimulant but it did not help, and an hour later the dolphin was dead. The conclusion they reached was that the dolphin may have been ostracized from the company of the other dolphins. When excluded this way dolphins become desperate. They attach themselves to anything or anyone, and sometimes allow themselves to die. Are not people equally sensitive and vulnerable? Do we not need other people? Is not this why God gave us the caring fellowship of the church, the body of Christ, the family of God, in which we feel each other's pain and respond to each others need?

139

I like these words by Henri Nouwen:

We can participate in the care of God who came,
not to be powerful but powerless,
not to be different but the same,
not to take away our pain but to share it.

Through this participation we can open our hearts
to each other and form a new community.

Let me close by sharing with you an example of a caring person.

For years one of the most powerful men in Washington was Speaker of the House Sam Rayburn. He had tremendous influence upon our country in the legislation he helped engineer.

One day he heard that the teenage daughter of a newsman had died. Early the following morning there was a knock on the reporter's door, and when he opened it he found Speaker Rayburn standing there. "I just came by to see what I could do to help," he said. The flustered, grieving father replied: "I don't think that there's anything you can do, Mr. Speaker. We're making all the arrangements." "Well, have you all had your coffee this morning?" Rayburn asked. The reporter said that they hadn't taken the time, and the Speaker quickly said that he could at least make coffee for them.

While he was working in the kitchen, the reporter came in and said, "Mr. Speaker, I thought that you were supposed to be having breakfast at the White House this morning." "Well, I was," said Rayburn, "but I called the president and told him I had a friend who was in trouble, and I couldn't come."

May we be surrounded by the love of Christ
Who cares.
May we be surrounded by people who care.

May we be people who care in the name of
Christ our risen Lord.

JESUS: DISTURBER AND HEALER

The Fifth Sunday of Matthew.
Matthew 8:28 - 9:1.

Everyone has seen the little sign provided for guests in hotels, "Do not disturb." The two demon-possessed persons in today's Gospel lesson had placed such a sign on the door of their lives. When they saw Jesus approaching, they cried out, "What have you to do with us, O Son of God? Have you come here to torment us before the time? Do not disturb us."

These two persons were standing in the very presence of the Son of God. They could have had the water of life for the mere drinking! They could have had the bread of life for the mere taking! Yet they cried, "Leave us alone! Do not disturb us!" They drew a circle around their lives to shut Jesus out. They made of their hearts two prison cells that Jesus was forbidden to enter. They preferred to stay in that prison with demons rather than open the door to the Redeemer.

Tormentor

"Have you come here to torment us . . . ?" they asked. This is not just the raving of a demented person. Some people are always resisting the presence of Jesus. To them He is a *TORMENTOR* Who stirs up a crisis in the soul.

Herod, for example, was afraid that Jesus would torment him, would interfere with his life, his place, his influence, his power, so he set out to destroy Him. There are still those who would destroy Jesus, because they see in Him the One Who interferes with their lives. They wish to do what they like, and Jesus stands in the way, so they would get rid of Him. To *many people Jesus comes as a TORMENTOR*.

Alcibiades, a young irresponsible Greek, once said to Socrates, "Socrates, I hate you. Every time I see you, you remind me of what I am and you make me feel ashamed of myself." Do not many hate Jesus for the reason? Why is it, for example, that many people never darken the door of the church? Is it not because they do not want to be disturbed? They do not want the disturbing presence of Jesus in their private lives. As T. S. Eliot wrote:

"Why should men love the Church? Why should they love her laws?

She tells them of Life and Death, and of all they would forget.

She is tender where they would be hard, and hard where they would like to be soft,

She tells them of Evil and Sin, and other unpleasant facts."

"What have you to do with us, Jesus? Do not disturb us!" In other words, "Mind your own business, Jesus. Leave us alone. Get back to Palestine. Climb back into the Bible. Get back into Church. Get back anywhere as long as You do not interfere with our way of life. You have no jurisdiction over us. Don't I have a right to live my own life? What have You to do with me, Jesus of Nazareth?"

This is the cry of sinful man.

Jesus came with the promise of rest. But He usually has to make us restless with ourselves and with our world before He can give us His rest. He is a persistent disturber.

A Persistent Disturber

How does He disturb us?

He disturbs us by what He is. We can compare ourselves to other people and feel that we are so much better than they are. But when we compare ourselves to Jesus, we see how far short we have fallen of what God created us to be.

Secondly, He disturbs us by showing us what we may become. When we stand in His presence, our first word will be, "I am not like Him," but our second will be, "But I *can* be like Him by God's grace. I ought to be like Him. I want to be like Him."

Jesus disturbs us thirdly by the call of human need. We cannot be in the presence of Jesus and be at rest, at peace, as long as there are people suffering. He disturbs us about the injustices of our social order, about world peace, world hunger, about the hatred and the sin in our lives. He makes us restless about these evils that we may give ourselves to the changing of them.

Why does Jesus disturb? For only one reason: to heal us. He is the Divine Disturber in order that He may become the Divine Healer. Just as a physician will break a crooked bone in order to set it straight, God may break a wrong spirit in us in order to give us a chance to possess the right spirit.

A Divine Alarm Clock

Few people like alarm clocks. They disturb our sleep, and yet, though we dislike being disturbed, we set the alarm. Why? Because each day we have new work to do, new opportunities to possess. And unless we are disturbed we will sleep our chances away. In describing the Transfiguration of Jesus, St. Luke writes, "When they were fully awake, they saw His glory" (Luke 28). We must be fully awake mentally and spiritually if we are to see and share in God's glory.

Sometimes Jesus is like a divine alarm clock. He disturbs our conscience. He keeps us from being satisfied in some unsatisfactory life, because He has a better way for us to live. He makes us dissatisfied with the good because He wants us to have the best. He shakes us out of our complacence because He has mountains for us to climb with wider and wider horizons.

What response are we to make to this disturbing Christ? When our Lord awakens us, what are we to do about it? This is the big question. It is not ours to decide whether we shall or shall not be disturbed. He disturbs whether we like it or not. But it *is* ours to decide what we shall do once we are disturbed. If an alarm clock rings in your room, it can awaken you but it cannot drag you out of bed. Whether you get up or go back to sleep depends entirely upon yourself. All Jesus can do is disturb us. This He does in a thousand ways. But having done this, He leaves the rest to us.

143

Our Response

Now, what response can we make? Broadly speaking, we can make one of two. We can either get up or go back to sleep. *The villagers in today's Gospel lesson took the latter course.* They were disturbed by Jesus — so disturbed that "they begged Him to leave their neighborhood." He was interfering with their business. They were afraid that He would cut down their profits. So they asked Him to leave. And don't we do the same?

Even today there are people who say to Jesus, "Go away! I want nothing to do with You. I like my sin, my alcoholism, my adultery, my fornication, my bad-temperedness and my pride. I have learned to live with it, and I don't want You around making me feel guilty."

Others say to Him, "Don't bother with me! Go away! I'm not worth it. I'm past being saved. There was a time, once, in my youth. But it's too late now. Go away and preach Your Gospel to someone else!"

I used to wonder why some people never darken the door of a church. I don't wonder so much anymore. There are many people who *want* to doubt, *want* to believe that there is no God, *want* to stay outside the church, because they don't want Christ to disturb their lives. Outside the church, they can lead unexamined lives. Inside the church, they will know that they have sinned. They will see what it cost God on the Cross to forgive them. They will realize the enormity of their sin. Easier, then, to remain outside! Easier to ban Jesus from their lives!

When He Leaves

And when we ask Jesus to leave, He leaves. "And getting into a boat He crossed over and came to His own city." *When He leaves we are left without light, without love, without hope, without peace, without meaning.*

In Dostoievski's novel, "The Brothers Karamazov," when Jesus comes back in a modern setting, He disturbs peoples' values so much that the Grand Inquisitor asks Him to leave! "Why have You come to disturb us?" he asks.

Jesus disturbed people then; He disturbs people today. The world has not changed much. We do not want to be challenged,

144

changed, confronted, altered, disturbed, awakened, redeemed or transformed.

Some of us will go along with Jesus up to a point. The point is reached when we discover that there is a cost — any cost — to following Jesus. Then we do not want Him around. We ask Him to leave.

The Divine Healer

But to the day we die, Jesus will be disturbing us. He will be disturbing us in our sin through guilt not so much to punish us as to awaken us to His forgiving love and to the peace of God that passes all understanding. He will be disturbing us by showing us what we may become through God's grace, i.e., sons and daughters of the Most High, heirs of His eternal Kingdom. He will be disturbing us through sorrow and suffering to lift our eyes to the things that are eternal. He will be disturbing us constantly by the call of human need. But always He will be disturbing us out of love as the physician disturbs the wound by cleaning it and stitching it that it may heal. He is the Divine Disturber only that He might better be the Divine Healer.

If it is within our power to resist our Lord when He disturbs us, it is also within our power to yield to Him. If we can say "no" to Him, we can also say "yes." And it is this yes that makes the difference between the spiritually victorious and those who go down in defeat; one yields to God's awakenings, the other does not. How great was the disturbance our Lord wrought in the heart of Paul on the road to Damascus. What a great awakening experience it was for Paul. Because of it Paul became one of the greatest and most victorious Christians who ever lived in this world. What He did for Paul, Jesus does for us. In countless ways, He tries to disturb us, to awaken us to a new and better life.

"Have you come here to disturb us?"

Yes! He has! For unless He disturbs us, unless He first convicts us of sin, who can be healed? Who can be saved?

145

PRAYER

What have You to do with us, Lord? Why, You have everything to do with us! You are our peace. You are the bread of life without which we cannot live. You are the water of life that satisfies fully the perennial thirst of the soul. You are the God "in whom we live and move and have our being." Come, then, Lord! Disturb us, if You will, to awaken us to new opportunities, to heal us, to save us. We are Your children. You have everything to do with us. You are our Lord and Master. Amen.

THE LIGHT BEGINS WITH ME

The Holy Fathers
of the Fourth Ecumenical Council.
Matthew 5:14-19.

The keeper of a lighthouse was boasting of the brilliance of his lamp. Asked what would happen if the lamp went out or if the reflectors became dull, he replied, "Impossible! Out there are ships sailing. If this light goes out tonight, someone will be shipwrecked."

In a similar way the eyes of the world are fixed on the followers of Jesus. For this reason Jesus said in the Gospel lesson today:

> *"You are the light of the world. A city set on a hill cannot be hid. Nor do men light a lamp and put it under a bushel, but on a stand, and it gives light to all in the house. Let your light so shine before men, that they may see your good works and give glory to your Father Who is in heaven."*

No Man Lives Unto Himself

Every person exerts an influence on the world. If you are not a Christian and are living a Godless life, by your example you are making it harder for others to follow the ways of peace and righteousness. By your unbelief, you are making it easier for some to reject the way of life through Christ Jesus.

It is a solemn thought that our lives are continually radiating light or darkness, and there are ripples of influence that we can never control or stop. No man lives unto himself.

No one is entirely without influence. Everything we say and do has a ripple effect. It either hurts or helps. It either leads or misleads. It either advances God's Kingdom or hinders it. We are responsible — and are held responsible by God — for the influence we are sending out from our lives.

147

A Cheap Candle?

You may think that your influence does not count for much and that the world will be little better or worse for your having lived. "I have no more influence than a cheap candle," someone once said.

"A cheap candle can do many things," his friend replied. "It can burn down a house. It helps me to read a chapter in God's Word. Let your cheap candle 'so shine before men that they may glorify your Father in heaven.'"

Reflected Lights of Christ

We are held responsible by God for the influence we send out from our life. If we elect to receive God's gift of salvation and become citizens of heaven, we become involved in the lifestyle of the kingdom. We become the reflected light of the Great Light, which is Christ. It may seem awesome, but the world will know Him because it knows us.

We may not shine brightly, and sometimes our lives may be only a glimmer of what they ought to be. But even so, if we are true followers of Jesus, our lives will be of the light and not of the darkness.

St. John Chrysostom has said:

"He (Christ) left us on earth in order that we should become like beacons of light and teachers unto others; that we might act like leaven, move among men like angels, be like men unto children, and like spiritual men unto animal men, in order to win them over, and that we may be like seed, and bear abundant fruits. There would be no need for sermons, if our lives were shining; there would be no need for words, if we bore witness with our deeds. There would be no pagan, if we were true Christians."

Light Planted In Us at Baptism

When I was baptized, I was illuminated. God lit His flame in my soul. He planted His light within me so that I may shine for Him in the world. "For it is the God Who said, 'Let light shine out of darkness' who has shown in our hearts to give

148

the light of the knowledge of the glory in the face of Christ''
(2 Cor. 4:6). God has planted His light in our hearts.
We read in the PHILOKALIA:

> *"When we are being baptized, our soul, purified
> by the Spirit, becomes brighter than the sun; not only
> are we then able to look at the glory of God, but we
> ourselves take on something of its radiance. As
> polished silver, illumined by the rays of the sun,
> radiates light not only for its own nature but also from
> the radiance of the sun, so a soul, purified by the
> Divine Spirit, becomes more brilliant than silver; it
> both receives the ray of Divine glory, and from itself
> reflects the ray of this same glory. Therefore the
> Apostle says, 'But we all, with open face beholding as
> in a glass the glory of the Lord, are changed into the
> same image from glory to glory'"* (2 Cor. 3:18).[1]

The Image of God Reflects His Glory

God made us in His image so that we may have the
potential and the capacity to reveal God to others when the
Trinity comes to dwell in us. St. Paul expressed this well when
he wrote to the Corinthians, ''You yourselves are our letter of
recommendation, written on your hearts, to be known and read
by all men; and you show that you are a letter from Christ
delivered by us, written not with ink but with the Spirit of the
living God, not on tablets of stone but on tablets of human
hearts'' (2 Cor. 3:2 - 3). With His Spirit God has written a letter
in our hearts for all to read. The light must shine!

Thus, made in God's own image and having received the
light of His glory in baptism, I am called to reflect that light in
my everyday life. Every time I come to church and light a
candle, I need to say to myself: ''God needs me to shine as a
candle for Him in this dark world. Help me, Lord, to shine for
You today not dimly but as brightly as possible that the world
may see my good works and give You glory.''

---

[1] "Writings From the Philokalia: On Prayer of the Heart," Kad-
loubovsky and Palmer. Faber and Faber. London. Copyright 1951. p. 166.

The divine light that radiated from Christ radiated also from His saints. St. Serafim of Sarov was seen by one of his spiritual children transfigured like a sun. St. Gregory Palamas from personal experience discusses the uncreated energies of God that come to abide in us when we open ourselves to God. We are so illumined, transfigured and transformed that our lives become like candles radiating the glory of God and illuminating the world's darkness.

The Purpose of Shining

The purpose of this shining for Christ is not that the world may see our good works and praise us, but that it may see God in and through our good works and fall down before His presence in our midst. Jesus is not promoting here a theology of good works, but a theology of the glory of God. That is why He says, "Let your light so shine before men that they may see your good works, *and give glory to your Father who is in heaven.*" All of our good works are not to get us glory, but to get God glory.

Jesus urges us not to hide our light "under a bushel" but to place it on a stand where we can give light to all. There are many kinds of bushels under which we hide the light—and they are all bad. There is the bushel of shyness. There is the bushel of pride. There is the bushel of indifference, the bushel of a cold heart, the bushel of a love that has died, the bushel of false humility. All these bushels are condemned by Jesus. They not only hide the light but they also extinguish it. The light is to be placed on top of the bushel where it can be seen by all.

Light Has Come To the Region of Death

When Christ came into the world, there was no light. When He left the world, there was no darkness. Matthew, quoting Isaiah, said of Jesus: "The people who sat in darkness saw the great light; and to them who sat in the region and shadow of death light has sprung up" (Matt. 4:16).

If after two thousand years, there is still a deep darkness in this redeemed world, it is because the light that is Christ flickers or shines through those who follow Him, through us. That is why Jesus commands us to let His light shine brightly through us: "Let your light so shine before men that they may see your good works and give glory to your Father who is in heaven" (Matt. 5:16). And that is why St. Paul pleads with us: "Once you were darkness, but now you are light in the Lord: walk as children of light, and try to learn what is pleasing to the Lord" (Eph. 5:8-10). If there is darkness in the world, it begins with me. If there is to be light in the world, it must begin with me.

Light Up the Candles!

During he most trying and desperate days of early American history, a man wrote a very pessimistic letter to Benjamin Franklin. He concluded it with the words, "The sun of liberty has set." The great old patriot who was not afraid of the dark wrote back, "Then light up the candles!"

Is not this the message of Jesus in the Gospel lesson today? "Light up the candle I placed in you at baptism. Make My Presence a reality, a living light, in your life and in some other life. Give of yourself to one dark soul with no conditions attached. Light a candle in the darkness." Let the Risen Christ dawn. And let the dawn begin with you.

The world is in darkness and it cries out to us with the words of that winsome reporter of World War II days, Ernie Pyle: "I wish you would shine any of your light in my direction. God knows I've run out of light." If the world has run out of light, why do we hide the light of Jesus under a bushel?

A Lost Child and the Beckoning Porch Light

Some years ago an urgent plea came over the radio: "Will all of you please turn on your porch lights. A small child has wandered away from home. The child is retarded and unable to speak. He loves porch lights and will probably come to someone's porch."

All over town, lights were turned on quickly. People sat quietly listening for a strange sound at their front doors. Then the announcer came on with a good word. The little boy had indeed gone to a lighted porch and his parents were on the way to pick him up. People felt happy that they had done something to help someone in need.

151

A long time ago Jesus looked out on a world dark in sin and death. He saw not just one little boy in need of a welcoming light; He saw countless millions alone, lost and dying, without a light to guide them home.

He Gave Them a Command

Then He looked at the faces of His followers as they sat on the mountainside and gave them the command: "Let your light so shine before men, that they may see your good works and give glory to your Father who is in heaven."

May the light of Jesus shine out of your two eyes like a candle set in two windows of a house, bidding all who are lost to come in out of the darkness of the storm.

For there is indeed a storm and darkness. And there are indeed wanderers, looking for a secure home and a place where the loneliness in their lives can be healed by love. You and I and all of us have the power to reflect to them the love of Christ.

Henri Nouwen said once, "It is very hard to keep your mind and heart directed toward God when there are no examples to help you in your struggles."

A Triumphalism of Good Works

The words of Jesus in today's Gospel lesson have something special to say to those in the Church who have a triumphalist attitude about their faith. They are the ones who pride themselves on saying, "We are the true Church — the Church of the Apostles. We have kept unsullied the deposit of faith given by Christ . . ." Jesus is telling us in today's Gospel lesson that if we have the true faith, we don't have to shout it to people. All we have to do is *do* what the true faith tells us to do. *Live* our faith, then people will see the product of our true faith, i.e., our good works and glorify our Father in heaven. Jesus urges upon us not a proud triumphalism of words but a humble triumphalism of good works which express the true faith and give glory — not to us — but to our Father in heaven. Works more than words are the magnet that attracts others to Jesus.

When asked why, although the battery was weak, the horn still operated loudly, but the car lights were dim, an auto

152

mechanic said, "It takes more power to make a light than to make a noise." More than people need noise, they need light and Jesus provides us with the power to be not clanging cymbals but lights.

I like what someone said about Christians: "They are people who punch holes in the world's darkness, building people strong enough to solve life's daily problems, and helping the world to be a little less deaf, a little less dumb, and a little less blind."

Get Rid of the Darkness That Is In You

One of the prerequisites for letting the light of Jesus shine through us is to get rid of the darkness that is in us, what some psychologists call the "shadow self." St. Paul identifies this darkness in us. He calls it "the works of the flesh: immorality, impurity, licentiousness, idolatry, sorcery, enmity, strife, jealousy, anger, selfishness, dissension, party spirit, envy, murder, drunkenness, carousing, and the like" (Gal. 5:19-21). Our task, as Paul tells the Christians in Rome, is to "cast off the works of darkness and put on the armor of light; let us conduct ourselves becomingly as in the day. . . . Put on the Lord Jesus Christ" (Rom. 13:12-14).

The areas of darkness in us need to be dealt with if we are to light up with the grace of Christ. Someone asked: What do a light bulb covered with mud, a window covered with soot, and a life spotted with sin have in common? The answer is: They are all incapable of allowing light to shine through them for the benefit of others. Regardless of how bright and pure the light, the net result will be darkness until the dirt is dealt with. The problem is not with the source of light, but rather with the vessel through which the light is shining. That is why Jesus warns, "If therefore the light that is in you is darkness, how great is that darkness!" (Matt. 6:23). Only a cleansed vessel will let the light shine brightly. That is why the true Christian reaches out daily for the Windex bottle of God's forgiveness. "If we confess our sins, He (God) is faithful and just, and will forgive our sins and cleanse us from all unrighteousness" (I John 1:9).

Live In the Sunlight of His Presence

In addition to removing the darkness of sin from our lives through daily repentance and confession, the second prerequisite for letting the light of Christ shine through us is to cultivate the presence of Christ in our lives and never to depart from that presence. As the instructions on a phosphorescent match case said, "If you wish me to shine, keep me in the sunlight." Picking up a dry, shrivelled leaf and discovering it to be amazingly fragrant, a weary traveller asked the leaf whence came this exquisite perfume and the leaf replied, "I have been for a long time in the company of a rose." It is the presence of Jesus that generates light in us. Seek out that presence constantly through regular prayer, Bible study and the sacraments and your life cannot but reflect the light of Christ through your good works.

Francis R. Line wrote of Francis of Assisi:

"Francis of Assisi was poor,
Frail in purse and body.
No excess possessions,
No surplus muscles or strength.
Plain sandals, rude cloak, rough cowl.
Not much to look at.

But
No one ever saw him when they looked.
They saw the One he reflected.
He was a mirror of Christ.

I conclude with these words by William Stoddard:

"You are the world's light."
"Who, me?"
"Yes, you."
"Isn't that a pretty big order, Lord, for an ordinary
guy? The world is huge and I'm not even
shining very well on my own street or in my
own home. I couldn't pull it off.
"I'm not asking you to be big enough to do the job.
Bigness doesn't count anyway—neither the
bigness of the world nor the bigness of your
light. It's faithfulness that counts. All the

darkness in all the universe can't conquer the
light of a single candle. I only ask you to
share my love and square with my truth—
then you can't help it, you will be the world's
light."
"Here am I, Lord, shine through me."

"GOD IS! I AM!
WITH HIM I CAN"

The Seventh Sunday of Matthew.
Matthew 9:27-35.

Napoleon would have erased two words from our vocabulary "I can't" and "Impossible." These are the same words Jesus came to remove from our vocabulary "I can't" and "Impossible." What Napoleon could not do, Jesus can.

When the two blind men came to Him in the Gospel lesson today asking to be healed, Jesus asked them, "Do you believe that I am able to do this?" They said, "Yes, Lord." Then He touched their eyes, saying, "According to your faith be it done to you."

I like these words by Nita Wolf:

> *"God is!*
> *I am!*
> *With Him*
> *I can."*

Listen to this inspiring one-liner: "Success comes in cans; failure in can'ts."

The basis for the removal of the two words "I can't" and "Impossible" from our lifestyle as Christians is first, the promises of God in Scripture, and secondly the power of God.

God's Promises of Power

First, let us look at the promises of God in the Bible:

"Is anything too hard for the Lord?" (Gen. 18:14).

"Is the Lord's power limited?" (Numbers 11:23).

"Behold, the Lord's hand is not shortened that it cannot save . . ." (Isaiah 59:1).

157

"Be strong in the Lord and in the strength of His might. Put on the whole armor of God, that you may be able to stand against the wiles of the devil" (Eph. 6:10).

"Ah, Lord God! It is Thou Who hast made the heavens and the earth by thy great power and by thy outstretched arm! Nothing is too hard for Thee, who showest steadfast love to thousands" (Jer. 32:17 - 18).

"Some boast of chariots, and some of horses; but we boast of the name of the Lord our God. They will collapse and fall; but we shall rise and stand upright" (Psalm 20:7 - 8).

"For I am not ashamed of the gospel: it is the power of God for salvation to everyone who has faith . . ." (Rom. 1:16).

"For the kingdom of God does not consist in talk but in power" (I Cor. 4:20).

"He is able to save completely all who come to God through Him" (Hebr. 7:25).

"He is able to do far more abundantly than we ask or think" (Eph. 3:20).

"He is able to help those who are tempted" (Hebr. 2:18).

"All things are possible to him who believes" (Mark 9:23).

"I can do all things through Christ who strengthens me" (Phil. 4:13).

The Power of God

All of these promises are based on God's power guided as it is by His love.

We have been created to live on the power God gives us just as an electrical appliance is built to run on the current of an electric power line. The manufacturer of an appliance assumes that electricity will flow into it and he designs all the parts

158

accordingly. If the electricity does not flow into it, the appliance is worthless. It is exactly the same with us. God has created us so that our whole being springs to life the moment we receive His power. Fullness of life becomes a reality for us when we have His power in us.

Jesus did not come to give us a new and more exacting set of rules to struggle toward; He came that we might have power and life, and have it to the fullest.

The Real Energy Crisis Is Within

The one word that characterizes people today is the word despair. Why despair? Because so many people do not have the power to deal with what life hands out to them. Our real problem is that most of us don't have the power to do what we know is right and the power to refrain from doing what we know is wrong.

In other words, the real energy crisis in the world is in you and me. Too many of us are cut off from our source of power because we are closing our lives to the ministry of the Holy Spirit.

We read in Acts 1:8, "You shall receive power when the Holy Spirit comes upon you." Jesus spoke these words to His discouraged and frustrated disciples. They reached for power, and it came down like the roar of a mighty wind and transformed them. They had a tremendous inflow of power through the Holy Spirit. They were overflowing with energy. They walked away from Pentecost and went to the ends of the world preaching, teaching and exemplifying Jesus in their lives. They started the greatest spiritual revolution in history. They became people of power through the Holy Spirit.

A Popular Word

Power is a popular word. Our language is full of it:

Knowledge is power
Money is power
A power struggle.
Willpower,
A world power
Black power.

159

The power of suggestion.
The power of positive thinking
Nuclear power.
A power structure.
Power to the people.

Despite the popularity of the word "power," most of us feel powerless. The reason for this is our failure to recognize the real source of power: THE POWER OF THE HOLY SPIRIT and THE POWER OF PRAYER.

His Power Is Sufficient

"The power of the Most High will overshadow you" the angel promised to Mary at the Annunciation. The power of the Most High — that's what we need and that's what God offers us. "You shall receive power when the Holy Spirit comes upon you." When we have this power, we know that the power behind us will always be greater than the task ahead of us.

St. Paul uses the word sufficient to describe God's grace: "My grace is sufficient for you: for my strength is made perfect in weakness" (2 Cor. 12:9). God's power is indeed sufficient. Every one of us who has ever been through trials and suffering knows that God's grace is sufficient. In fact our weakness gives God an opportunity to show us how powerful He is and how sufficient His power is. Someone said, "The worst jolt most of us ever get is when we fall back on our own resources." But in our weakness we discover God's strength which is more than sufficient. When we have nothing but God, for the first time we become aware that God is enough. As St. Paul says. "Not that we are sufficient unto ourselves . . . but our sufficiency is of God" (2 Cor. 8:5). "And God is able to make all grace abound toward you; that ye, always having all sufficiency in all things, may abound to every good work" (2 Cor. 9:8). William A. Ward testifies:

> *God's strength behind you,*
>   *His concern for you,*
>   *His love within you, and*
>   *His arms beneath you are*
>   *more than sufficient for*
>   *the job ahead of you.*

But there are many people who feel powerless and insufficient to the tasks of life. "What can I do?" they say. "I am nothing. I am a zero." And my answer is, "I agree with you. I am a zero, too. But God is Number-One, and when I place Him before the zero, He is the one who gives meaning, value and power to the zero. Without Him, I am nothing; with Him, I am everything. Without Him, I am helpless; with Him, I can do all things. Without Him, everything is impossible; with Him all things are possible.

The Need to Be Connected

We cannot have power unless we plug into it, unless we connect to the source of power. As Bishop Northcott once wrote, "Nothing gets anywhere until it is connected. A horse never pulls until it is harnessed. A Niagara does not produce power until it is tunnelled. Steam never drives anything until it is channelled. No human life ever produces until it is connected with the power of God."

Just as when the nerves leading from the head are no longer connected to the legs, the legs become paralyzed, so it happens to many Christians. They allow themselves to be cut off spiritually from the head, who is Jesus. They disconnect themselves from the Body of Christ, the Church. The result is a paralyzed and powerless life. They need to make that connection to Christ through faith and the Eucharist that will release God's power into their lives.

Examples of God's Power

Let us look at a few examples of how God's power has helped people.

The Prophet Isaiah gives a superb example of God's power when he writes:

Have you not known? Have you not heard?
The Lord is the everlasting God, the Creator of
the ends of the earth.
He does not faint or grow weary, his understanding
is unsearchable.
He gives power to the faint, and to him who has
no might he increases strength,

161

Even youths shall faint and be weary, and young
men shall fall exhausted;
but they who wait for the Lord shall renew their
strength, they shall mount up with wings
like eagles,
they shall run and not be weary, they shall walk
and not faint.

(Isaiah 40)

The great Russian novelist Boris Pasternak tells of the tortures he endured in the Soviet Union for expressing his Orthodox Christian faith in his writings. Life was made into a hell for him. He tells where he received the power to endure: "I couldn't have made it but for Jesus, the Christ," he said. *"He came to me."*

He Came To Me!

"He came to me." This is the source of our power. Jesus comes not only to empower us with a future hope in the words, "I will come again to receive you unto myself," but He comes again and again to reveal Himself to us in the here and now. "I will come to you. . . . I will not leave you an orphan. . . . Even in the valley of the shadow of death. I am with you." He comes to us in our weakness to raise us up in power.

He came to a father who lost his son in an accident. He said, "When I first heard of my son's death, I felt there were three courses open to me. I could give way to despair. I could try to drown my sorrow in drink. Or I could turn to God. I turned to God and found in Him the power to overcome and transcend my grief."

I conclude with the testimony of a wife waiting for her husband to undergo major surgery after a serious accident:

On the morning of Erling's surgery, a violent
summer storm erupted. Storms are rare in southern
California, and in August rain of any kind is un-
usual. On that Saturday just two days after Erling's
accident, winds of hurricane force whipped the
coastline into snarling fury.

162

I sat alone in the sheltering quiet of the hospi-
tal corridor waiting for Erling to be wheeled from
Intensive Care to surgery when without warning all
the lights went out. Only the glowing exit signs
relieved the darkness. Immediately my thoughts
went to those patients, my husband included, who
were dependent on electrically powered machinery
for the maintenance of their vital functions—heart
monitors, stomach pumps, respirators, dialysis
units.

Before I had time to really explore the full
implication of this loss of power for Erling's im-
pending surgery and for all those other lives, the
lights flickered once, came on at half their power,
and then flared brightly once more.

Later I learned that when the storm disrupted
the normal flow of power, the hospital's own
generators began functioning, and this alternate,
emergency source of energy took over almost im-
mediately.

In much the same way, I think Erling and I
were operating on an alternate source of power
after the accident, power which is always available
but too often reserved only for the stormy days of
our lives.[1]

This woman — Marge Wold — had experienced God's
power and it was more than sufficient.

"Jesus said to them. 'Do you believe that I am able to do
this?' They said to Him, 'Yes, Lord.' Then He touched their
eyes, saying, 'According to your faith be it done to you.'"

When there is this kind of power loose in the world, why
do we spend so much time in pursuit of lesser kinds of power?
Why?

---

[1] "What Do I Have To Do — Break My Neck?" Erling and Marge
Wold. Augsburg Publ. Co., Minneapolis, MN. 1974. pp. 111-112.

PRAYER

Lord, help me to
be strong in you
and in the strength
of your might (Eph. 6:10).
For truly nothing is too
hard for you.   Amen.

"YOU GIVE THEM SOMETHING TO EAT"

The Eighth Sunday of Matthew.
Matthew 14:14-22.

A woman from Russia was visiting New York City some years ago. She maintained a stoic "Ours is better" attitude through a tour of Lincoln Center, the Empire State Building, and a cruise around Manhattan. Then her hostess took her to a supermarket. The veneer of smugness cracked as the Russian woman stood amid seemingly endless aisles of fresh vegetables, red meat and frozen foods. She had never seen anything like it before. She broke down and wept.

This may be true, but as someone said jokingly, "America has more food to eat than any other country in the world and more diets to keep us from eating it."

The Greatest Threat

The force that poses the greatest threat to international order today is not the Soviet Union, not the Islamic world and not inflation. None of these. "The most potentially explosive force in the world today is the frustrated desire of poor people to attain a decent standard of living." So says the report of the Presidential Commission on World Hunger.

Dr. Robert Coles, Professor of Psychiatry at Harvard University, says, "I can't think of any problem more serious for men, women, and children of this world than that of food — its aching absence for millions and millions of human beings, in every continent."

Jesus and Hunger

Jesus addressed this number one problem of the world in the Gospel lesson today when He ordered His disciples to feed

165

the hungry multitude: "You give them something to eat," He said.

Commenting on these words of Jesus, Stephen Neill wrote:

"Jesus is much concerned with loaves and fishes and other very material entities. He tells us that we are not to take anxious thought about such things. But, though He reminds us that man shall not live by bread alone, He never for a moment doubts that man shall live by bread. 'Give ye them to eat' still stands as His command to His Church. If at any time the Church has been inclined to spiritualize this command, to think that it has fulfilled its duty by providing man with spiritual food and so preparing him for life in heaven as a compensation for poverty and hardship on earth, the word of Christ is there to rebuke it." [1]

"You give them something to eat." Church members who deny their responsibility for the needy in any part of the world are just as guilty of heresy as those who deny any major article of the faith. To refuse to feed the hungry is in itself a denial of a major article of the faith of Christ.

"You give them something to eat." How right Berdyaev was when he said, "The question of bread for myself is a material question, but the question of bread for my neighbor is a spiritual and a religious question."

"You give them something to eat." Ghandi said once, "There are so many hungry people that God cannot appear to them except in the form of bread." There is a story which says that when God decided to visit the earth, He sent an angel to survey the situation. The angel returned and reported that most of the people lacked food. Then God said, "I will go but I will become incarnate in the form of food for the hungry."

So He came as the Bread of Life.

But, as Diane Ramsey writes, people, especially those who are well fed, are sick and tired of hearing about hunger today:

---

[1] *"Christian Faith and Other Faiths,"* Stephen Neill. *Oxford University Press. New York, NY. 1970. p. 155.*

I get so tired of hearing about
Hunger all the time.
Everywhere I go
Someone has to spoil
Everyone's pleasure by bringing
up the topic of hunger.

People have always been hungry
somewhere or another.
And it will always be so.
The Bible tells us so.

If there was something I could do
I wouldn't be so upset but I
cannot make a difference.
Not just me!
One person!

So why does television have
to display such awful
pictures just about the time
I sit down to enjoy my dinner?
It sure can ruin a good steak!

I guess this pretty much describes most of us today, but don't fret! We do not intend just to talk about the problem. There are many things we can do to become part of the answer to this number one problem of hunger. Here are some:

Jesus Must Feed the Hungry Through Us

1. If Jesus is to feed the hungry, He must do it through us. A person tells of seeing on the street one day a little girl cold and shivering in a thin dress, with little hope of a decent meal. He became angry and said to God, "Why did You permit this? Why don't You do something about it?"

For a while God said nothing. That night He replied quite suddenly, "I certainly did do something about it. I made you!" *"You give them something to eat."*

Jesus was able to feed the five thousand because there were people in the crowd who were willing to bring Him whatever little food they had: five loaves and two fish. Jesus sends none

167

away empty except those who are full of themselves; those who are unwilling to share.

The disciples determined their resources — five loaves and two fish. We, too, should start by taking inventory. Most of us have far more than five loaves and two fish.

God can work miracles if we are willing to bring to Him our five loaves and two fish. Frank Buchman once said, "Suppose everybody cared enough, everybody shared enough, wouldn't everybody have enough? There is enough in the world for everyone's need, but not for everyone's greed."

St. Augustine wrote,

*Find out how much God has
given you and from it take what
you need; the remainder which
you do not require is needed
by others.*

*The superfluities of the rich
are the necessities of the poor.*

*Those who retain what is
superflous possess the
goods of others.*

St. Basil wrote,

*"He who steals clothes (or food) from the poor is
a thief. He who has clothes (or food) and does
not clothe (or feed) the naked (and hungry) is
also a thief"* (bracketed words are mine).

We read in the early Christian (1st Century) document "The Didache":

*"Share everything with your brother. Do not say
'It is private property.' If you share what is
everlasting, you should be that much more
willing to share things which do not last."*

Listen to St. Gregory of Nyssa:

*"All things belong to God, Who is our Father
and the Father of all things. We are all of the
same family; all of us are brothers. And among
brothers it is best and most equal that all inherit
equal portions."*

168

Fasting

2.   In addition to sharing what we have, another way we can help feed the hungry is through fasting. It has been estimated that if the rest of the world ate the way Americans do and used as much petroleum in growing food as we do, the known world resources would be used up in less than 30 years.

We need to fast more than we do and to use the proceeds of our fasting to feed the hungry. One church in Texas decided that for every pound they lost, the members would give one dollar for world hunger.

We need to heed the words of the Prophet Isaiah:

"Is not this the fast that I choose . . .
   Is it not to break your bread with
        the hungry,
        and bring the homeless poor into
        your house;
   when you see the naked to cover him . . ."
        (Isaiah 58:6-7).

Gather Up the Leftovers

3.   In addition to sharing and fasting, a third way to help feed the hungry is by being less wasteful. In John's version of this miracle we read, "And when they had eaten their fill, He (Jesus) told His disciples, 'Gather up the fragments left over, that nothing may be lost'" (John 6:12).

The striking thing is that Jesus did not leave the leftovers scattered around. His power to feed the multitude did not tempt Him to be careless or to presume to waste God's gift of precious food. We're not told how Jesus used the twelve baskets full of leftovers. For that we can use our imagination. What we do know is that Jesus treated food as a precious gift.

Our modern "throw-away society" can learn something from the apostolic "gathering-up society." It has been said that your garbage disposal probably eats better than do 30% of the people of the world. A study revealed that Americans toss in the garbage cans as much as ten billion dollars worth of edible food every year. In just one restaurant in New York City the owner says they dump at least ten pounds of butter and one hundred pounds of meat each week. That amounts to two-and-a-half tons of meat and one-quarter ton of butter each year. Wasted. In just one restaurant. The waste of food and consumer goods in our nation is sinfully appalling.

If we could but become a gathering society, a conserving people, a preserving force instead of a wasteful one, the miracle of there being enough left over for all might well occur again in our time.

4. In addition to sharing, fasting and conserving, there is another way to help with world hunger. We just said that the greatest threat to the stability of the world is not nuclear weaponry but hunger. Yet the world continues to spend $750,000 every minute for arms. A true response from us to God's love would show itself in our using the same ingenuity in feeding the starving that we now use in making deadly missiles or easy-open beer cans. For example, the estimated $40 billion cost of the new MX missile would feed 50 million malnourished children. It would also build 65,000 health care centers and 300,000 primary schools.

Examples of What Can Be Done

Here are some simple examples of how we as Christians can respond to the command of Jesus: "You give them something to eat."

One person keeps track of what she spends for grain to feed the birds and she sends an equal amount to CARE. "It's not fair to feed birds," she says, "if you don't feed people." Think of this when you feed your dog next time.

In St. Paul, Minnesota, guests coming to a wedding were asked to bring gifts for world hunger rather than wedding gifts for the bridal couple. A total of $1,644.00 was raised for world hunger.

In Orlando, Florida, a couple celebrating their 25th wedding anniversary asked well-wishers to give for world hunger rather than gifts to them.

One person writes, "I believe giving up one main meal a week should be the minimum response. One Sunday a month could be designated for receiving the money which is set aside weekly. By giving up the meal, we would understand more personally the plight of the hungry and the scale of the crisis."

Another person carries around with him what he calls a "justice envelope." Whenever he buys a treat like a candy bar, he notes its cost and places the amount in his "justice envelope." Every so often he donates the contents of the envelope to his church for world hunger.

"Why do you call it a 'justice envelope?'" someone asked him. "Why don't you call it a 'charity envelope?'"

He replied, "Because I don't believe there is such a thing as charity. What do I have that God didn't give me? If I give a little of my surplus to someone less fortunate, I'm not giving a gift. I'm paying a debt."

The Bible says that at the Last Judgment people will ask Christ, "When did we see you hungry?" We are seeing one-fourth of the world's people hungry at this moment. Let us never say we did not know how much suffering there was. And there are so many little things we can do to help. The world's hunger for food must be relieved by our hunger for righteousness. *"You give them something to eat."*

A Parable

Many years ago the Lord of life encountered a tree along the side of a dusty road.

"Tree," said the Lord, "I have given you soil and water and sunlight all these many years. I have kept you safe from the storms. I have blessed your growth. Now I am tired and hungry. Have you anything for me?"

The tree answered back, "I have nothing for you, Lord."

From that day forward, the Lord withheld his blessing and the tree died.

Many years later, the Lord of life encounters one of His people along that same hot, dusty road. "Christian," says the Lord, "I am your creator. I have given you life. I have watched over you and given you food. I have blessed your days. I have enlarged your family and prospered your household. I have shown you mercy and grace. I have loved you and kept you in my love. Look around you. My world is hungry and broken. People in it are weary and in need. Have you anything for them?"

171

How do we answer the Lord?

PRAYER

We can't forget the amazing thing you did, Lord
with five loaves and two fish.
You fed thousands.
You multiplied our puny resources
and had a semi-load of leftovers.
May we not forget the boy who shared his fish.
He just had two. But he shared them.
Thousands benefited.
What do I have to share, Lord?
My bread, my fish, my possessions.
They are not to be grasped and hoarded.
They are to be shared and offered.
Then, and only then, can you multiply them.
Do your multiplying miracle through me.

—George White

SURVIVING
THE STORMS OF LIFE
The Ninth Sunday of Matthew.
Matthew 14:22 - 34.

When talking long distance to his sister in Minnesota, a person had a tendency to brag about the fantastic climate in Southern California. During one conversation, he couldn't resist mentioning a strawberry he had just picked from his garden that morning. "It's almost five inches around," he boasted. "Not bad for December." There was a pause. Then his sister replied, "You may be picking strawberries there, but back here in Minnesota we are walking on water."

The Gospel lesson today tells about Jesus walking on water. His disciples were in trouble on Lake Galilee, being tossed about mercilessly by the waves and the wind. "And in the fourth watch of the night He (Jesus) came to them, walking on the sea." Let's look at this story to see what it has to tell us about the storms of life and how to survive them.

Developing A Philosophy About Storms

First, no one should go through life without developing a philosophy about storms. You mean there is a philosophy about storms? Yes! Storms are to toughen wood. Storms are to plow up the earth. Storms are to test human beings. Storms are hard, but the one great thing about them is that they toughen and build life. A person was looking for the toughest kind of wood available. He found it on the top of a mountain. That's where the storms hit hardest. That's where the trees in resisting the powerful winds develop deep roots and solid wood.

Who has not faced storms in life? The storm of temptation, the storm of failure, the storm of sorrow, the storm of sickness? Jesus came to save us not *from* storms but *in* the storms of life. Storms may batter us physically, mentally, emotionally and

173

spiritually. But in the midst of their fury, Jesus is present to help us rise above them. He says to each believer, "Take heart, it is *I:* have no fear."

Rising Above the Storm

We can learn much from the way the eagle meets a storm. As the storm sweeps in, the eagle sets his wings at the proper angle so that the winds will pick him up and lift him above the storm. While the storm is hitting the earth, the eagle is soaring above it, using the very winds of the storm itself for propulsion.

God compares His people to eagles when He says, "They that wait upon the Lord shall renew their strength; they shall mount up with wings as eagles" (Isaiah 40:31). We face many storms in life: illness, opposition, failure, disappointment, but when they come, we can set the wings of our faith in such a way that the adverse winds will lift us above the storm.

PASSING THROUGH

"When Thou passest through the waters,"
Deep the waves may be, and cold,
But Jehovah is our refuge
And His promise is our hold;
For the Lord Himself hath said it,
He the faithful God and true;
"When thou comest to the waters,
Thou shalt not go down, but through . . ."

—Annie Johnson Flint

Storms Test Us

While it is true that storms come to strengthen us and that God gives us the strength to pass through them and rise above them, it is also true that storms come to test us. Phillips Brooks uses the analogy of a ship at sea, fighting a gale. The winds howl, and the waves roll. Will the ship hold together? It is a terrific struggle. But, really, the battle was fought long before, in the forest where the timbers grew, in the shipyards when the nails were pounded in and the planks laid and the seams caulked. The battle was fought in the care given through the

174

years in guarding against dry rot and broken ribs and loose fittings. *THE STORM IS MERELY THE TEST;* the battle was fought and either won or lost long before. Even men don't build their ships for calm weather and placid seas. Still less does God.

Not Alone

While the disciples were on the boat encountering the terrible storm, they must have felt terribly abandoned. They were left to themselves to struggle with it all. Jesus was away praying on the mountain. The waves were getting higher and higher. The night was dark. They were frightened, exhausted, soaked to the skin. They felt it was the end for them. But at the critical moment Jesus came to them, restoring safety, sanity and peace.

"He Came to Them"

In the hour of acute need, Jesus came to His own. *"He came to them."* He comes to storm-tossed souls today, and His presence brings the same miracle. The wind is stilled; courage returns; calm is restored. For the storms that sink us are not outside our boats but inside our souls.

St. Augustine said once, "He came walking on the waves; and so He puts all the swelling tumults of life under His feet. Christians — why be afraid?"

We do not have to endure the storms of life *ALONE!* In the hour of the disciples' need Jesus came to them. When the wind was strong and the waves rolling, Jesus was there to help. He comes to us today in the storms of life, with hand stretched out to save and with His calm, clear voice bidding us be of good courage, and not to be afraid. No person need struggle alone! "He came to them."

How beautiful the words of Edward Hopper:

Jesus, Savior, pilot me
Over life's tempestuous sea;
Unknown waves before me roll,
Hiding rock and treacherous shoal;
Chart and compass come from thee;
Jesus, Savior, pilot me.

175

It was a deep water sailor, Captain J. Rogers of the Merchant Marine, who wrote this beautiful paraphrase of the Twenty-Third Psalm:

The Lord is my Pilot, I shall not drift,
He lighteth me across the dark waters.
He steereth me in the deep channels.
He keepeth my log.
He guideth me by the Star of Holiness for
    His Name's sake.
Yea, though I sail 'mid the thunders and tempests
    of life, I shall dread no danger; for Thou art
    with me.
Thy love and Thy care they shelter me.
Thou preparest a harbour before me in the
    Homeland of Eternity.
Thou anointest the waves with oil, my ship rideth
    calmly.
Surely sunlight and starlight shall favour me on the
    voyage I take, and I will rest in the port
    of God forever.

He Walked On the Raging Waves

The presence of Jesus restored peace not only to the waves but also to the troubled souls of the disciples. "My peace I give to you," said Jesus. We can have that indestructible peace, if we will call out to Him to come to us in the storms of life.

Jesus,
walk on the boisterous waves
of my life.
Speak "peace"
to the angry billows
of self.
Be with me
in my little bark
and bring calm
where confusion
has been created
by contrary winds
                    —D. Buitendyk

176

Calm In the Midst of Storm

A little girl asked her father, "What was God doing last night in the storm?" Then, answering her own question, she said, "I know. God was making the morning."

He does this for us in our storms. He prepares the peace and calm of the morning. Let me give you an example.

Many years ago eleven Communist leaders were on trial in New York for conspiracy to overthrow the government by violence. The trial dragged on for eight months, and was presided over by Judge Harold Medina, who showed an almost superhuman patience. The behaviour of the Communists was abominable. They harassed the judge in every way, trying to break down his will in order to obtain a mistrial. Along about the seventh month, Judge Medina felt he was going to pieces. His nerves were frayed by constant bickering, telephone calls threatening his life, and the lives of his loved ones. He was on the verge of collapse. Listen to his testimony:

"One day I had to leave the court room. My head suddenly began to swim. I recessed the court and walked quickly to the little room at the back and lay down. I felt panicky, and I'll be frank about it, I was certain that I could never go back. I had stood as much as a human being could endure. I knew I would have to quit. But suddenly there in the little room I found myself like a frightened child calling to his father in the dark. I asked God to help me, just to take charge, that His will might be done. I cannot report anything mysterious or supernatural, there was no vision or visitation, all I know is that as I lay on the couch some new kind of strength flowed into me. I was in that little room for only fifteen minutes, but that brief communion with my God saved not only the trial but my sanity as well. I opened the door and walked again to the bench with a firm realization that I could take whatever was ahead."

Jesus calmed the storm that was raging in this honorable judge's soul. He restored his soul and strengthened him powerfully for the task ahead. Can He not do the same for us?

It's A Ghost!

When Jesus came walking on the storm-tossed sea that night, the disciples did not recognize Him. They thought it was a ghost. And they cried our in fear. But Jesus calmed them, "Take heart, it is I: be not not afraid!"

When the waves of life roll high, when adversity, suffering and death break in upon us, we often fail to recognize Jesus. We stare at these ghosts until our hearts tremble with anxiety. Someone once said that when we die, Jesus will at first appear to us to be like a ghost and we shall be frightened. But then as He draws closer to us with the words, "Take heart, do not fear: it is I," we shall see not a ghost but our beloved Savior.

"It Is I, Be Not Afraid"

When the storm was fiercely raging
On the Lake of Galilee,
And their helpless bark was tossing
On the wild tempestuous sea,
Walking on the raging waters
In a robe of light arrayed,
Jesus came, oh, hear Him calling —
"It is I, be not afraid!"

When the storms of life are raging,
And the night is long and drear,
When our strength is spent with toiling,
And our spirits sink with fear,
Oft again we see Him coming,
Swiftly hast'ning to our aid;
Oft still we hear Him calling —
"It is I, be not afraid!"

When the night of death shall lower,
And the Jordan's surges roll,
When the hour and power of darkness
Overwhelm the sinking soul,
Then above the raging billows,
And night's deepest, darkest shade,
We shall hear Him calling to us —
"It is I, be not afraid!"

—A. B. Sompson

"Lord, Save Me!"

When Peter began to sink into the waves, he cried out, "Lord, save me!" It was a short prayer. Someone said that if he had prayed longer, he would have drowned. He said, "Lord, save me" and the Lord did. Jesus reached out, took his hand, lifted Peter back up, and together they walked on the water back to the boat.

When you know you're going under and you feel a big hand take hold of you and pull you up, that's God. Every time in your life when you've been going under, and strength was poured into you and you were lifted up, that's God. That's God pulling you up.

For, you see, Jesus Christ is unsinkable. He fought death where death is king — in a tomb — and He has won. He has broken the power of death. He has given us eternal life which is indestructible. It will not sink in the sea of time. "In Him was life, and the life was the light of men."

Keeping Our Eyes On Jesus

"And Peter answered Him, 'Lord, if it is You, bid me come to you in the water.' He said, 'Come.' So Peter got out of the boat and walked on the water and came to Jesus; but when he saw the wind, he was afraid, and beginning to sink, he cried out, 'Lord, save me.'" As long as Peter keeps his eyes on his Master, he walks fearlessly over the waters of the lake. But as soon as he takes his eyes off the Master and looks at the wind and the waves, he begins to sink. As long as we keep our eyes on Jesus, our feet will go where they are supposed to go. The moment we take our eyes off Him, we're in trouble.

I won't look back; God knows the fruitless
    efforts,
The wasted hours, the sinning, the
    regrets;
I'll leave them all with Him who
    blots the record,
And mercifully forgives, and then
    forgets.

179

*I won't look forward; God sees all
    the future,*
*The road that, short or long, will
    lead me home.*
*And He will face with me its every
    trial.*
*And bear with me the burdens that
    may come.*

*But I'll look up—into the face of
    Jesus.*
*For there my heart can rest, my fears
    are stilled;*
*And there is joy and love, and light
    for darkness,*
*And perfect peace, and every hope
    fulfilled.*

—Annie Johnson Flint

PRAYER

Oh, the storms that sweep down on me, Lord! The winds and rains of adversity, guilt, hurt, misunderstanding, failure, insecurity, hardship, tension, hollowness, doubt, rejection—they pummel me like hailstones in an open field. I feel so threatened, lost and alone. Save me, Lord, or I perish.

But there is salvation with you, for you can still the storms and bring me tranquility. Help me to relax, relax, relax in your care and keeping.

I know you've got the whole world in your hands, including me, and that nothing will happen to me except it passes through your knowledge and will.

Be my shelter and preserver through every storm and bring me by your strong hand to the place of peace, through Him who is my peace, Jesus Christ my Lord. Amen.

—T. Wersell